FLICKER
TO
FLAME

Living with Purpose,
Meaning, and Happiness

JEFFREY THOMPSON PARKER

Morgan James Publishing • New York

FLICKER TO FLAME

ISBN: 1-60037-108-6 (Paperback)
ISBN: 1-60037-107-8 (Hardcover)
ISBN: 1-60037-109-4 (eBook)
ISBN: 1-60037-110-8 (Audio)

Published by:

MORGAN · JAMES
THE ENTREPRENEURIAL PUBLISHER
www.morganjamespublishing.com

Morgan James Publishing, LLC
1225 Franklin Ave Ste 325
Garden City, NY 11530-1693
Toll Free 800-485-4943

Habitat
for Humanity®
Peninsula
Building Partner

Cover and Interior Design by:
Michelle Radomski
One to One Creative Services
www.creativeones.net

IN MEMORY OF JUANITA PARKER
Your love, hope, faith, kindness, and courage
continue to inspire us. We all miss you.

THIS BOOK IS DEDICATED TO MY FAMILY.

To my wife, Laura, and my children Rachel, Jessica, and Ryan.
You make my life complete and provide me an
abundance of purpose, meaning, and happiness.

To my dad, Tom.
Your work ethic and generosity still continue to teach me.

I love you all.

ACKNOWLEDGEMENTS

DURING THE WRITING OF this book, I had the truly fortunate chance of meeting Jay Conrad Levinson, a celebrated author and father of "Guerilla Marketing." Jay, your affirmation of my work and encouragement to publish this book filled me with both inspiration and motivation. As you have written, "All writers need allies" and I am deeply grateful to have had you on my side. Thank you.

As a first time author, transforming an idea into a book requires the help and experience of professionals. My editor, Amanda Edmonds, is the professional who provided me with the help and experience required to make this book a reality. Amanda, without you this book wouldn't be what it is today. Thank you.

The images presented throughout the book, which assist in conveying the message, were created with the help of a talented graphic artist and friend, Nate Trueblood. Thank you.

PRAISE FOR
FLICKER TO FLAME

"Reading *Flicker to Flame* filled me with both inspiration and enlightenment, not to mention exhilaration. It is nearly biblical in its timeless wisdom as well as a delightful read. Thomas Jefferson referred to the pursuit of happiness. In this remarkable book, Jeff Parker gives wings to that pursuit."

JAY CONRAD LEVINSON
Author of *Guerrilla Marketing* series of books
over 14 million sold, now in 41 languages

"Jeff Parker hits an inspiring "how-to" grand slam with *Flicker to Flame*. *Flicker to Flame* will ignite your passion and creative juices while providing a concrete and fluid process for personal and professional success."

WILLIAM SINUNU
Author of *Life Could Be Sweeter—101 Great Ideas
from Around the World for Living a More Rewarding Life*

"Compassionate action is our reason for being on this Earth. *Flicker to Flame* helps you find the path to that spiritual truth. We all seek to live in a climate of joy, and in this inspiring book, Jeff Parker wonderfully describes the way to that which we seek."

DR. CHUCK DIETZEN
Founder and President, Timmy Foundation

"Impressive. Enthusiasm and passion flow from Jeff Parker through *Flicker to Flame* to the reader. *Flicker to Flame* is chocked full of sound and inspiring advice and as a culture we can certainly use more life affirming material."

STEVE TIMM
Professor and playwright, DePauw University

"*Flicker to Flame* is a well organized read that provides direction and hope that a life with purpose, meaning, and happiness is possible. Jeff Parker provides a manageable, easy to follow approach on successful living. How to get the most out of life is presented step by step in this book that will change lives.

MELANIE HART
President, Tsuchiya North America

"Every journey begins with the first step; Jeff Parker's *Flicker to Flame* is a great first step in the journey of understanding and enlightenment."

RICK MIRACLE
Co-author of *Trolleys and Squibs*

"Reading *Flicker to Flame* provides a way to reach the pinnacle of what life has in store for each of us. The incorporation of Jeff Parker's Nine Axioms of Happiness into practiced habits will help lead to a successful life filled with joyful experiences."

JERRY YEAGLEY
Indiana University men's soccer coach 1973-2003
Six NCAA Championships, NCAA Division I record 544 wins
Member National Soccer Hall of Fame

ELEMENTS

INTRODUCTION

———◦《◉》◦———

"FLICKER TO FLAME" WAS written to help others, as well as myself, further understand and explore the meaning of happiness. It is my assertion that this exploration of happiness contains the necessary elements to lead us to discover our own personal definition of the meaning of life. The exploration and the eventual enlightenment that is possible will assist us in living with happiness, purpose, and fulfillment. T.S. Eliot wrote, "We must not cease from exploration. And the end of all our exploring will be to arrive where we began and to know the place for the first time."

Happiness is defined in the dictionary. However, the academic definition does not truly define such a wide, diverse, and complex concept. The concept of happiness is one to be defined by the individual and really requires a personal interpretation. How one person defines happiness will to be quite different from how it is defined by just about anyone else. We all possess our own treasure maps on the voyage of life which provide us with direction toward personal happiness, and these maps, like our definition of happiness, are personal and unique.

The purpose of "Flicker to Flame" is to examine the principles, natural laws, and axioms that when practiced will place us in the pursuit of happiness. The Nine Axioms of Happiness, as they are identified in the book, are universal, natural laws which are common to all prosperous civilizations. These are not concepts that I invented—just compiled—and described in a way that I hope is clear and concise.

To be in the pursuit of happiness, which allows us to achieve the most out of life, we must work with the universal, natural laws that deal with happiness, in this case, the Nine Axioms of Happiness. How we apply these axioms to our lives will vary greatly depending on our unique abilities, talents, and strengths. Learning, understanding, and putting into daily practice these axioms will fundamentally change lives and facilitate the pursuit of happiness.

Our Creator has bestowed upon us a tremendous gift. The gift with which we are presented—the awesome opportunity of a flicker—comes with a responsibility. We have been entrusted to let our light shine, to fulfill the purpose of our light, and to live the life intended. Whether our light remains a flicker, or is coaxed and nurtured into a bright, shining flame is our choice. Living the Nine Axioms of Happiness will deliver the tools necessary to let our light shine like a flame, and to live happy, healthy, productive lives filled with joyful experiences. Oh, what a joyful life is possible when we are able to transform flicker to flame.

I welcome you to the pursuit. I will warn you that even though the axioms are simple to understand and seem like common sense, they are difficult to put into daily practice. It will be a constant struggle, as it is for me, because the more you learn and know, the more you see how long the road really is. Learning and not doing is not true learning. Knowing and not doing is not true knowledge. If you will prepare yourself to learn and put into practice your new-found knowledge, your mind will be opened to a whole new realm of possibilities.

I make a solemn promise to you that developing the Nine Axioms of Happiness into a lifestyle will allow you to realize your dreams and change your life from mundane to magnificent. Remember, bring your loved ones along with you, and be assured that you are not alone in the journey.

PASSION STATEMENT

My passion is sharing the concepts in this book, which have been revealed to me, with you. The Nine Axioms of Happiness are given to help produce lives with purpose, meaning, and happiness. In sharing these concepts, I hope you are able to realize your dreams, transform your life from mundane to magnificent, and give thanks to our Creator for your blessings. If we apply these concepts to our lives, together we can assist humanity in its quest to develop a higher, divine-like level of consciousness.

May learning and understanding create joy and happiness in your life.

1

VISION
The pursuit of happiness

———— »«◎»« ————

"Happiness is the meaning and purpose of life,
the whole aim and the end of human existence"
—Aristotle—

MANKIND'S STUDY OF AND search for understanding about happiness has existed for thousands of years. The topic of happiness has been studied and written about by every culture, civilization, and religion. Our desire to be happy is part of our nature, how we are designed. The 18th century German philosopher Immanuel Kant, regarded as one of the great thinkers of his time, wrote, "Happiness, though an indefinite concept, is the goal of all rational beings."

Before we go any further in our exploration, we need to highlight an important distinction within the concept of happiness: the distinction between momentary and purposeful happiness. Momentary happiness is superficial and based on sensation and pleasure. It is happiness that is fleeting, the sort of happiness you feel when someone tells you a joke, you see something amusing, or experience sensual pleasure. It may put a smile on your face for a while, but it does not stand the test of time. Hence, it is momentary happiness. Momentary happiness plays an important role in our lives, and there is a time and place for a discussion of momentary happiness. But that time and place is not in this book.

In "Flicker to Flame" the type of happiness we are referring to is purposeful happiness. Purposeful happiness is a sense that our lives have meaning, and that we are involved in fulfilling a worthy purpose. It is happiness that is derived from a spiritual source, which is fed by the satisfaction of pursuing what defines us.

An important prerequisite to pursuing purposeful happiness is understanding what defines each one of us. If we can truly understand our traits—and it is these traits or gifts that constitute the flicker instilled within us by our Creator—then we can begin walking the path towards purposeful happiness.

Here is a partial list of some attributes and gifts that we as individuals possess: sense of justice, quest of knowledge, seeking of power, honor, generosity, sense of family, independence, physical activity, social involvement, and romance. Each individual possesses a combination of attributes and gifts. By identifying these characteristics, the transformation of flicker to flame begins; we must understand who we are and then strive to utilize these characteristics. By working with the flicker instilled within us and growing the flicker into a magnificent flame, which will provide a light for the entire world to see, purposeful happiness will be delivered into our lives.

An example of the difference between momentary and purposeful happiness and how it relates to living a more fulfilling life can be found in the life of Malcolm X. When his dream of becoming a lawyer was curtailed due to racial discrimination, he re-directed his energy toward a life of seeking gratification in the arena of drugs and sex. By the age of 21, he was addicted to drugs and sent to jail for burglary. His attempt to find happiness in the pleasurable, sensual experiences of life was not producing happiness; for he was not involved in a cause he deemed a worthy purpose. He had experienced momentary happiness but not purposeful happiness. Adrift on the sea of life and going nowhere, he reached out to the Nation of Islam and its teachings for direction. Upon discovering his passion for greater social justice—his flicker—his thoughts and actions provided direction for others and he soon developed a following. As a leader, he experienced more stress and anxiety and less pleasure, but he was blessed with far more happiness. His thoughts and actions were in tune with his calling, and he was able to exchange his pursuit of momentary happiness for a pursuit of purposeful happiness which gave his life greater meaning. His transformation from flicker to flame was dramatic. I never met Malcolm X, and this book was written more than 40 years after his death. Nonetheless, after researching his life and transformation, I am confident that he understood and put into practice some, if not all, of the Nine Axioms of Happiness.

Here is a formula, written as an equation, for transforming your flicker into a flame:

Awareness of Gifts + Nine Axioms of Happiness = Purposeful Happiness

Happiness requires work, energy, effort, and awareness. The search for happiness leads to inner peace, fulfillment, success, and contentment, which are some of the rewards of this life. Consequently, misery or unhappiness requires little or no effort. It is easy to see the bad, the negative, or unfairness in this world or in our lives. The importance of happiness to our very existence is summarized by the Dalai Lama, the head of the Dge-lugs-pa order of Tibetan Buddhists, who won the 1989 Nobel Peace Prize. He said "I believe that the very purpose of our life is to seek happiness. That is clear. Whether one believes in religion or not, whether one believes in this religion or that religion, we all are seeking something better in life. So, I think, the very motion of our life is towards happiness..."

Happiness is a higher state than misery. We are designed for personal growth as well as designed to test the boundaries of this existence, to tap into our incredible reservoir of resources in an attempt to become an outward example of our inner greatness, and to let our light shine as bright as possible. One of our responsibilities or duties should be to strive personally to reach a higher level of understanding and enlightenment, and ultimately to contribute to the elevation of our human community to a higher state.

One of the paradoxical battles of this human existence is our innate drive toward continual improvement which is in conflict with our desire to take the path of least resistance. We see something and want to improve it; we study something and want to expand our knowledge of it. Simultaneously, we seek the easy way. The pursuit of happiness is not the easy way. It is a personal and arduous journey which leads to understanding and enlightenment, and contains special rewards during the quest. Conversely, misery—the simpler way—loves company, provides no growth, and gives no rewards.

The pursuit of happiness requires that we envision ourselves engaged in the activities that make us happy, which provides us with a sense of purpose and direction. By envisioning the pursuit of happiness, we will produce a sense of meaning and give continuity to life. The vision will give us a target to aim for and a reason for our existence. The motivation to transform ourselves and to live with an abundance of purpose, meaning, and happiness resides within our vision.

The Declaration of Independence, penned by the founding fathers of the new, emerging United States of America, is one of the greatest documents ever written. This document contains very precise language regarding the relevance of happiness.

> *"We hold these truths to be self-evident, that all men are created equal, that they are endowed by their Creator with certain unalienable Rights, that among these are Life, Liberty and the pursuit of Happiness—That to secure these rights, Governments are instituted among Men, deriving their just powers from the consent of the governed—That whenever any Form of Government becomes destructive of these ends, it is the Right of the People to alter or to abolish it, and to institute new Government, laying its foundation on such principles and organizing its powers in such form, as to them shall seem most likely to effect their Safety and Happiness..."*

—Declaration of Independence

The founders of the United States of America possessed insight, enlightenment, and understanding, not only in regard to the governing of people but also with respect to the needs and rights that we all strive to attain. They comprehended the intricacies of human nature. They understood that ingrained in all of us exist undeniable truths that all humans seek. The founders also understood the insight offered by Thucydides, an ancient Greek historian and author, who wrote: "The secret of happiness is freedom. The secret of freedom is courage." Their perception that we all desire to live, to be free, and to be happy was extremely accurate. The founders understood the importance of happiness to the human spirit. In fact, it is so important that the right to pursue happiness is prominently and specifically mentioned in the Declaration of Independence, one of the most powerful documents written by man.

"Flicker to Flame" is presented to provoke thought and to inspire personal reflection, so that each of us may improve our lives and set the pursuit of purposeful happiness into motion. On the journey, discovery of what is important and meaningful in life will be revealed. Changes, improvements, and the accomplishment of dreams and goals are some of the experiences that will be encountered during the voyage.

Success is an over-used and misinterpreted word. It is important not to confuse the acquisition money and wealth or the collection of possessions with the definition of success. Instead, happy people are successful people: Happiness = Success. If we love what we are doing, if we are working towards growing our flicker into a flame, we will be happy.

Imagine being in a cold, damp forest; you will need a fire for warmth, cooking, and security. The fire is started but barely burning, and is in danger of going out. There is wood available; it's easy to get because it's scattered around the forest floor, but the wood that is easy to access is too large and wet and would extinguish the small, emerging fire. The barely visible fire needs to be coaxed and encouraged with a proper fuel source, such as small, dry kindling. When the effort is put forth to acquire the proper fuel source by chopping away the wet exterior and exposing the dry, useful kindling, the flicker will then begin to grow into a useful bonfire. A flicker, when coaxed to grow with the proper fuel source of the Nine Axioms of Happiness, will also turn into a bonfire of genuine success and purposeful happiness that will be seen throughout the dark forest. Others will be drawn to the light and warmth of the impressive fire and will seek to understand how the wonderful, useful fire was created. They will want to learn how to transform their own small, currently useless flickering fire into one that is both magnificent and useful.

People who discover their gifts and pursue their passions are often rewarded financially. However, monetary gain is usually not their passion; if it is, they are on the wrong path. If your passion pursuit does produce financial gains, careful attention to the accumulation of wealth and all the ramifications that accompany it is required. Wealth should not become a distraction from the passion. Be aware and keep passion as the proper focus. Don't lose the love or understanding of the passion and get knocked off course in the pursuit of happiness.

In "Flicker to Flame," our definition of purposeful happiness has three parts: first, to create the opportunity to pursue passions that contain a purity of cause; second, to conduct the pursuit at your discretion; and, third to experience the joy the pursuit produces. If we can find a way to do the things we love to do and, moreover, are able to do them for the right reasons, to follow our own time schedule, and to appreciate the rewards of the fruits of our labor, we will be living with purpose, meaning, and happiness.

The transforming of our flickers to flames will change our existence from mundane to magnificent and deliver an abundance of happiness into our lives. Once we each understand our flickers and make a commitment to pursue happiness, action is the next step. Even if the action is small, it is a step toward fulfilling destiny. The first step is sometimes the hardest one. Even though it may be difficult, it is movement toward a vibrant, exciting life in which we fulfill the goals and dreams that define us.

There is nothing new in this book. I divulge no secrets, and I describe no tricks. What is contained in this book are just observations that I hope you can absorb and infuse into your life.

"I invent nothing; I rediscover."
—Auguste Rodin

If we are ready, by reading, understanding, and implementing the axioms into our lives, we will begin to experience results that have only existed in our dreams. Through the discovery of our true selves, we will accomplish lofty goals, produce outstanding results, and undergo a metamorphosis that leads to a content, inner peace. The quest will take active and continuous effort on our parts. The life-long journey will lead us to experience supreme happiness. This euphoric state is not a place where you dwell; it is an experience that is ever-changing. So, be vigilant in your pursuit and be aware of the opportunities life will present to you.

If the time is right in your life to receive the message contained in "Flicker to Flame" and you are ready to become acutely aware of the principles contained in this book, you will begin to move toward a more fulfilling life. As your life improves and you are creating happiness, you will become a magnet. People will sense your supreme happiness and will be drawn to you because you live a satisfying life, and this satisfaction will radiate from you. Your responsibility is to assist others who are close to you in their pursuit. You cannot make them happy—that's their job—but you can help them by providing the necessary principles. Each time we admit another to the culture of happiness and joy, we all gain, and humanity prospers. Let your pursuit of happiness begin.

2

GENESIS
Begin at the beginning:
Evaluate and identify passions

————— ⋙《◉》⋘ —————

*"Only passions, great passions
can elevate the soul to great things."*
—Denis Diderot—

When you tell your story, which is the condensed version of your life and the way you define yourself to the world, you are describing passions, both past and present. The important things in life that each one of us has accomplished as well as those toward which we are striving add quality to life. Our flickers—the endowed gifts, talents, and callings which reside within us—need to be recognized before they can be coaxed out of hibernation. By both becoming acutely aware of the flicker which is a part of our being and by understanding that the expression of these gifts is our destiny, we will place ourselves at the genesis of transforming our lives from mundane to magnificent. Evaluating and identifying the passions which define us is the first step in living a life with purpose, meaning, and happiness. Discovering passions instilled in us by our Creator and securing an opportunity to make them come true is a key component to purposeful happiness.

THE PURSUIT: UP CLOSE AND PERSONAL
Dan is one of the partners of a large, profitable construction company. He and his partners have designed and built office buildings, commercial

complexes, and upscale residential communities. The company and Dan personally have received numerous awards for their designs and buildings from trade associations and organizations, both private and civic. The company is well respected throughout the region by contractors, vendors, and customers for their quality and professional work as well as for their civic pride.

Dan lives in large, lovely home which is tastefully landscaped, has a manicured lawn, and is exquisitely furnished. He and his family drive the latest, trendy vehicles, have a vacation home in Florida, and go on vacations to far away, exciting places.

Dan seems to have achieved what many people can only dream of achieving. Outwardly, Dan gives off the illusion of success. However, inwardly Dan is unfulfilled for he lacks purpose. He is only going through the motions of life and experiencing an ordinary existence.

The combination of Dan's apparent success and internal dissatisfaction is indicative of the internal struggle between his practical self and his true self. Our practical self is primarily concerned with how the world perceives us, how much money we make, or what kind of car we drive. The true self, on the other hand, is concerned with personal growth and development. The practical self is concerned with doing, while the true self is concerned with being.

Dan believes he has a purpose and is struggling to uncover what it is. As he begins to let go of his practical self and begins to search for his true self, he will discover his calling. After much soul searching, he rediscovers his lost passion for studying, learning, and understanding ancient cultures and history, a passion which extends to understanding how the application of lessons from the past can help humanity today. In school, he always loved to study history and actually took part in an archeological dig while in college. Just the thought of this experience brings a smile to his face. Dan comes to the realization that his passion, his calling, his purpose was to understand the ways of ancient cultures and civilizations and to pass along that knowledge to the people of the 21st century—to be a conduit of knowledge from the past to the present.

Dan is at the genesis of his journey towards happiness. He has uncovered his passion and believes his studying, understanding, and eventual teaching of the ways of ancient cultures is part of the reason of his existence. Now that Dan has performed this vital task of evaluating and identifying a passion, it is time for the implementation of the Nine Axioms of Happiness. As Dan learns, understands, and becomes proficient in the practice of these nine principles, the meaning of his life will become clearer, and he will begin to experience happiness, fulfillment, real success, and inner peace: the fruits of the Nine Axioms of Happiness.

Dan's calling was a lost passion, waiting to be rediscovered. In your own genesis, begin by evaluating unfulfilled dreams. Wishes, dreams, and callings are buried within us, buried by the distractions of an ordinary existence. We can't escape the internal nagging of an unfulfilled dream; this is because we are destined to be or do what we are meant to be or do. The sooner we realize that fulfillment of our destiny is the way life is meant to be, the sooner purposeful happiness will be showered upon us. Focus, pray, concentrate, or meditate about the passion hibernating within you, waiting to be realized and shared with the world. To make dreams come true, we must unleash the incredible vast internal resources with which we have been blessed. As we turn a passion pursuit into a priority and begin viewing, believing, and behaving as if we are living the dream, before we know it, the dream becomes reality.

Romans 12:6–8 describes the concept of flicker with which we are endowed, as well as what to do with our flicker: "⁶We have different gifts, according to the grace given us. If a man's gift is prophesying, let him use it in proportion to his faith. ⁷If it is serving, let him serve; if it is teaching, let him teach; ⁸if it is encouraging, let him encourage; if it is contributing to the needs of others, let him give generously; if it is leadership, let him govern diligently; if it is showing mercy, let him do it cheerfully." It is our destiny to discover our passions and apply our best effort as we strive to see them to fruition. Understanding our gifts and pursuing the fulfillment of them will place us on the path toward realizing the magnificent life intended.

Purposeful happiness is possible when each of us see ourselves as a powerful force of nature pursuing our mighty cause. Faith in our cause and the securing of opportunities that abound is crucial for our crusade to advance. If we wait for the world to give us what we think will make us happy, we will be waiting forever. Our charge is to lift a torch with the flame of destiny fulfilled for future generations to see, and to pass on the torch before we die. If we are successful in living the life we are intended to live, purpose, meaning, and happiness will be our companions.

Only a very few fortunate people who follow their calling, who are blessed with talent, who are pursuing their passion for the right reason, and who apply an exceptional work ethic to their pursuit are financially rewarded. The outside world may perceive these fortunate ones to be lucky or simply in the right place at the right time. The outsiders see the money or materials produced and confuse wealth with success. Contrary to the superficial perception of outsiders, these fortunate ones are blessed because they have discovered the true meaning of supreme happiness. Yes, they have accumulated wealth; however, their wealth is not the source of their happiness. Seek out these people—they will have a content, inner peace and will seem happy—for they know where they are going and have insight. If we take the time to listen and analyze what they reveal to us, it will be of assistance in our own pursuits. These enlightened ones will probably speak in clichés and metaphors; seek to understand and read between the lines because they are communicating important information and clues. There is meaning in their words that will assist us in maximizing potential.

Most people just exist and are not on passion pursuits. However, that doesn't mean we cannot strive to be counted among the fortunate ones. The fortunate ones are those who, in addition to having found their calling, loving what they do, and doing it for the right reason, have discovered how to transform their existence into a passion pursuit and are possibly being rewarded by making a life out of following their dreams.

An example of a fortunate one is an athlete who loves her sport and couldn't image doing anything else; she would play even if she wasn't getting paid. She is a fortunate one because she is able to play the game she loves and, at the same time, she understands why she is making the most of her talent and, because of her passion and talent, is getting paid to play. She has created happiness in this one aspect of life, her professional life.

Another example of a fortunate one is a woman who is at home raising, shaping, and developing her children. She is the key to running a loving household for her family. As a partner, friend, and confidant to her husband, and a nurturer, caregiver, and mentor to her children, her destiny is being fulfilled and she understands why. The pursuit of purposeful happiness is underway in many aspects of her life. Her aura of happiness radiates from her, and it assists her loved ones in their pursuits. The words of Gelett Burgess illustrate fortunate ones' understanding of the world: "There is work that is work, and there is play that is play; there is play that is work, and work that is play. And in only one of these lies happiness."

Passions, callings, and dreams are reasons why people start businesses, create works of art, raise their children, write books, cure diseases, and build monuments. If we are keenly aware of our passions, then we will be ready to strike when the opportunity to turn a dream into a reality is presented. We must keep dreams alive because we never know when the magical collision of a prepared dream and opportunity will occur. The fulfilling of a dream may happen any time during our life, so keep in mind the words of George Eliot: "It is never too late to be what you might have been."

If you understand your major passions, are actively pursuing them, and the pursuit is producing the desired results, this implies that nothing in your life needs to be changed or improved. If this is the case, stop reading this book; you are in the pursuit of happiness, and you may even be experiencing supreme happiness.

Passions, working together like gears, drive the pursuit of happiness.

Minor passions are the activities that we should be involved in when not pursuing our major passions. Minor passions are not distractions and should not be a hindrance to our goals. Minor passions should be rejuvenating hobbies that lend support to overall well-being.

The absence of passions, callings, and dreams will lead to an ordinary existence. The definition of ordinary existence is a life full of mundane distractions, which cause one to live with a lack of purpose, meaning, and happiness, and to not truly experience all that life has to offer. Ordinary existence is just going through the motions, adrift on the sea of life in a rudderless boat going nowhere. We all have gifts waiting to be exhibited before the world. We also possess the ability to overcome ordinary existence by following our passions and securing an opportunity to be actively involved in their fulfillment. Everyone has something to offer the world—a purpose, a reason for existence. It is by uncovering and living our calling that we will be propelled through ordinary existence and into the world of possibility and abundance.

Once ordinary existence has been identified, each individual must determine if this type of existence is sufficient. If it is not and, instead, a desire to live with purpose, meaning, and happiness is internally expressed, then we must learn to execute perspective variation to energize the transformation. Perspective variation is changing the way we currently see things. We have the ability to vary our perspective, to see the world in a different light. It is like getting a new prescription for the glasses through which we see life. By viewing the change we hope to achieve and by seeking a new bold approach to make it come true, an uplifting, exhilarating experience will soon be born.

Attitude will dictate whether we are happy or sad, a victim or survivor, as well as how we interpret whatever life has in store for us. We have all heard the old adage: When given lemons, make lemonade. There is a reason why this saying has become an old adage. To create joy, it is important to vary the perspective through which we view the incidents of life, both large and small. In changing perspectives, we will develop an attitude that expects and searches for happiness. As we learn to find the good and the positive, we will soon find ourselves with more contentment and inner peace. An attitude of abundance gives life to passions, callings, and dreams. With the proper attitude, there is no stopping us from achieving that which is intended for us. Life contains many uncertainties and provides no guarantees, and what happens to us in life is filtered through our attitude. Our attitude can allow us to fulfill our destiny or it can hold us captive in an ordinary existence. Remember, we each possess the remarkable ability to control our attitudes which, in turn, controls the degree of happiness we will experience.

Dan, the unfulfilled designer/builder, was able to execute perspective variation by changing the way he viewed success. For him, success changed from having things to pursuing his love of learning about and understanding ancient civilizations. By varying his perspective of his life and world, which required substantial changes in his life, Dan placed himself at the beginning of the pursuit of purposeful happiness. He expects to embody the change he has envisioned.

The responsibility of happiness rests squarely on our own shoulders. Common sense tells us that if we hate the things we are doing, no matter what aspect of our lives is involved, the results are going to be unpleasant and negative. Common sense also tells us the converse is true. If we love what we are doing, despite the inevitable ups and downs, the results are going to be positive because we are pursuing our passions, doing the things that make us feel alive. Discovering our gifts and getting in tune with our flicker is the genesis for living the extraordinary life intended for us. The path of purposeful happiness begins with each individual and the gifts with which he or she has been blessed.

The writing of a passion statement following the realization of ones' flicker is like adding small, dry kindling to an emerging fire. By clearly defining a dream and giving it life through the written word, the journey toward purpose, meaning, and happiness will begin. A passion statement that is specific and attainable will act as a port in the storm when the clouds of doubt and lost focus begin rolling in. This tangible representation of a life imagined will provide motivation and create an awareness to seize opportunities which will be offered. Things don't happen by accident.

The commitment to transform flicker to flame takes courage. Stepping out of a current comfort zone and plunging into the unchartered waters of pursuing purposeful happiness is not an easy thing to do. It is much easier to talk, wish, or hope about what we are going to do than to actually do something about it. Most people have convenient excuses about why they haven't done something yet. There's always tomorrow; or, someone or something is holding them back. Each of us has only scratched the surface of our tremendous potential. Instead of settling for the path of least resistance, we must make a commitment to test the limits of our personal boundaries. In doing so, we will cause the flicker to begin to grow. Defining your passion, making a commitment to yourself, and becoming actively involved in pursuing your purpose will give meaning to your life.

Engaging our unique talents, strengths, and abilities in order to expand our individual flicker will cause a sense of satisfaction and fulfillment, as we enjoy doing what comes naturally. Rather than spending time and effort to develop skills for which we have no real aptitude or interest, we are better off trying to work with our God-given strengths. If naturally a nurturing, giving person, try to incorporate these strengths into everyday life and work—for instance, as a caregiver. If curious and inquisitive, develop the talents for research and teaching. We all have unique strengths which we bring to life. If we uncover and develop our passions, a happier, more satisfying life is in store. Living the life intended and giving thanks for our gifts is described in Matthew 5:16: "Let your light shine before men that they may see your good works and give glory to your father who is in heaven." As our lives become a shining beacon revealing the way to purposeful happiness, we will inspire others who see the light to begin their pursuits of purposeful happiness. If enough lights are created, a higher divine-like level of consciousness is possible.

By evaluating and identifying passions, callings, and dreams, and by securing a chance to live life in pursuit of these passions, we will create an opportunity to experience more joy and happiness.

3
THE NINE
AXIOMS OF HAPPINESS

The Nine Axioms of Happiness have been revealed to help produce lives with purpose, meaning, and happiness. The Nine Axioms deliver a plan of action to help realize dreams and transform lives from mundane to magnificent. Envision a worthy purpose as a rocket. To launch a rocket, a fuel source is required. The reading, understanding, and implementing the Nine Axioms of Happiness will deliver the fuel necessary to launch lives into the orbit of extraordinary.

Exploration of potential leads to enlightenment.

There is no hierarchy for the Nine Axioms of Happiness, for no single axiom is more important than another. They are presented and numbered one through nine, but there is no linear progression. Once you discover your worthy purpose—your flicker—move to applying the axioms as opportunities arise, and eventually you will begin to experience purposeful happiness. As with any skill or learned behavior, there is a learning curve involved in the successful practice of the Nine Axioms. The chapters are self-contained and designed so that it is easy to reference or read about any one axiom without needing to have read the prior chapter.

As we become aware of the axioms, natural gravitation towards the ones with which we are more comfortable will occur. However, we must seek to understand, become proficient, and weave all Nine Axioms of Happiness into the fabric of life. If we can accomplish this, an exquisite tapestry of purpose, meaning, and happiness will have been created.

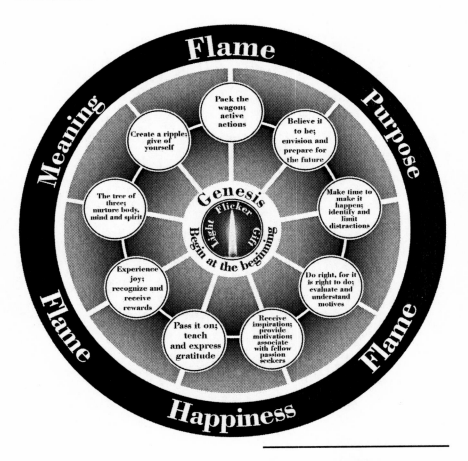

The path of flicker to flame travels through the Nine Axioms of Happiness.

FIRST
AXIOM OF HAPPINESS
Pack the wagon
Active actions

———◦《◉》◦———

"Whatever you can do, or dream you can, begin it.
Boldness has genius, power, and magic in it."
—Johann Wolfgang von Goethe—

Oliver was a sharecropper on the Dawson farm. Oliver also had a dream, a vision of providing a better life for his family. He wanted his kids to be able to receive a better education than he did and to be able to fulfill their purpose in life; he didn't want them to be chained down, scratching out a living on someone else's farm.

Even though Oliver and his family were just getting by, there was a certain amount of security in working the Dawson farm. The small cabin they called home did provide some protection from the elements, and they did have food on the table. There would be risks if they left the farm and tried to make it on their own.

After much thought and prayer and discussion with his wife Hannah, Oliver decided the rewards for his children were worth the risks they would incur. They heard of some land in the southern part of the state that was for sale on contract. It wasn't the rich farmland they worked on the Dawson spread—it was hilly country with trees. But with the native hardwoods, at least they could build themselves a real home. It would a tough living, but it held the promise of a better life for the children of Oliver and Hannah. The decision was made.

A spectacular sunrise greeted Oliver that early November morning. The reddish, purple haze of the sunrise not only contained all the colors of the prism, it also contained all the possibilities of a new beginning. Excitement filled the air on the frosty autumn morning. It was moving day. "Pack the wagon!" Oliver triumphantly proclaimed. It was time to begin actively pursuing his dream of providing a better life for his family.

It was the first step, of many yet to come, of actually doing something toward the pursuit of his dream. Hannah could see the joy in Oliver's eyes, and the children also understood the importance of the command. Those simple words "pack the wagon" contained a special message the children would always carry with them, the idea that happiness follows you when you are living a dream.

Happiness follows when the wagon of destiny is
packed with enthusiasm and persistence.

The pursuit of happiness requires active actions. Once our purpose has been revealed, we must get involved in doing something to make it happen. Benjamin Disraeli said this about action and happiness: "Action may not always bring happiness, but there is no happiness without action."

Commitment to action is an essential element to become our ultimate selves. To experience the life we have imagined or to achieve a significant goal which gives meaning to our lives, daily strides toward those ends are required. We are unique beings, one of a kind, like a fingerprint or DNA strand. Our experiences and situations are unique as well, which means there is no predestined course to follow in order to achieve a life full of purposeful happiness. For each of us, our dreams and our vision of our intended life require our full, undivided attention and active actions if we are going to make them come true. For us to arrive at our envisioned destination, our actions must be specific, focused, and real.

While transforming active actions into a way of life, we mustn't be afraid of making mistakes. Errors are unavoidable. What's important is to continually strive towards our goal. Learning and enlightenment will be gained from trying and failing and trying again. We must be willing to learn from mistakes, and move on. In basketball, a coach can tolerate a hustle foul, an error that resulted from a player who was aggressively trying to make something happen.

Even though this is a unique journey that each of us has undertaken, and there is no exact script to follow, it does not mean we are alone. There are other trailblazers ahead of us, and they have the ability to provide us with assistance and guidance if we are willing to seek them out and understand their message. While actively pursuing our passions, we will each cross paths with fortunate ones. Trusting our instincts will allow us to figure out who they are. It is important to learn from them concerning how and why they were able transform their lives. As we gather information along the way, we will add it to the formula we are developing.

Keep active and experience the joy of small successes, for it is rejuvenating. Keep commitment strong by drawing upon the faith that fulfilling our God-given abilities will deliver the life envisioned. Do not let naysayers become an anchor and slow down progress. It is not easy to make the most of potential. Passion pursuits require concentration, focus, and a sustained effort. It takes time, love, and sacrifice to exhibit the great gifts we have inside us. Sometimes the results we produce can prove to be astonishing; they may provide an example or be an inspiration to a single individual or to entire generations. Michelangelo wrote this about the effort required when pursuing talents: "If people knew how hard I worked to get my mastery, it wouldn't seem so wonderful after all."

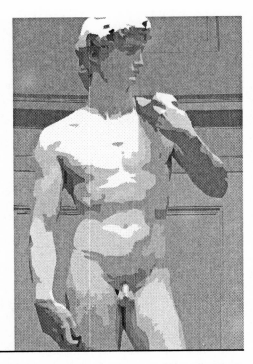

Transforming vision into reality requires commitment and sustained actions.

Keep active; hard work is its own reward. There will be tedious and unpleasant tasks associated with the pursuit. However, we shouldn't focus on these minor issues, but rather view them as part of the overall process of living the dream. The self-confidence gained in completing tedious tasks will be a welcome companion during the voyage of life.

Once a passion is uncovered and the active actions toward making it real begin producing results, dramatic and uplifting changes will begin to appear. Assuming responsibility for our own happiness is a liberating experience that will also create positive changes. If commitment is strong enough and an exceptional work ethic is applied, there is no preventing our goals from being realized. What a joy it is to be involved in a passion, to be engaged in a calling, to be actively fulfilling a purpose larger than ourselves, and to be on the path of understanding the whole aim of our existence.

The active pursuit of passions
leads to victory over mundane existence.

Keep active, stay focused, and make daily progress toward realizing the dream. Progress may be manifested in a multitude of ways: planning, thinking, making contacts, completing tasks, preparing, experiencing joy, helping, learning, and the list goes on and on. Life is too short and we have a limited amount of time to fulfill the dream that yearns inside each of us. Let's not miss the opportunity to be or do what each of us is supposed to be or do. Horace wrote in the "Odes," "Carpe diem, quam minimum credula postero," Latin for, "Seize the day, put no trust in tomorrow." Do not procrastinate and put off what needs to be done today. Do it now and keep your momentum moving forward. Focus on what it is going to take to accomplish the current goal, the necessary actions required to further progress the dream. Motivation should be strong, as involvement in active actions is part of making goals and dreams come true.

Harvest and enjoy the fruit from the tree of life
as it becomes ripe. Procrastination may let the fruit spoil
and not be enjoyed as it is intended.

Actively pursuing our passions will put a smile on our faces. Our work, our efforts should be an inspiration to the ones around us. The enthusiasm and the joy our active actions are producing should be obvious. The contrary is also true. If we are working or are involved in a situation that is not a passion (something that is drudgery) this will also be obvious to the world. We will never reach supreme happiness unless we change the situation with perspective variation or uncover a passion. Kahil Gibran wrote, "Work is love made visible. And if you cannot work with love but only with distaste, it is better that you should leave your work and sit at the gate of the temple and take alms of those who work with joy."

Reaching a goal, maximizing abilities, and pursuing a passion require effort and determination. We have the ability within us to create the lives we have envisioned, to produce the results we desire, or to become the personification of our dream. Dreams are always delivered gift-wrapped with the ability to make them come true. The effort required to open the present is up to you.

Remain active and determined to reach the goal. Expect continual bombardment of negativism by people who doubt destiny can be fulfilled. The more we hear we cannot do it, the stronger our resolve should become. Use the world's doubts as motivation. View the negativism as fuel for the passion pursuit locomotive. Once a passion pursuit locomotive pulling rail cars loaded with determination starts rolling and gathers speed, it is difficult to stop.

Create a plan of action. Outline specifically what needs to be done to reach the destination. Learn while involved in active actions, and adapt the plan as knowledge is attained. Be confident in actions and be clear in the intended goal. To be effective, actions must be specifically directed toward the envisioned goal.

W. Beran Wolfe eloquently communicated the concept behind "pack the wagon" with, "If you observe a really happy man you will find him building a boat, writing a symphony, educating his son, growing double dahlias in his garden, or looking for dinosaur eggs in the Gobi desert. He will not be searching for happiness as if it were a collar button that has rolled under the radiator. He will not be striving for it as a goal in itself. He will have become aware that he is happy in the course of living life twenty-four crowded hours of the day."

Time is the currency of life.
Spending it on purpose, meaning, and happiness
fulfills destiny.

The Pursuit: Up Close and Personal

Dan, the unfulfilled designer/builder who we witnessed uncover his passion in Chapter 2, has taken actions towards pursuing his actual dream. After much thought, prayer, and consultation with his family, Dan has entered into discussions with his partners about selling his interest in the business so that he can return to school and pursue his education in his chosen field. These actions will require radical lifestyle changes for Dan and his family such as moving and adjusting their spending habits. Dan has begun to pack the wagon and can already sense a change toward a more fulfilling life.

FIRST AXIOM OF HAPPINESS
Pack the Wagon... In a Nutshell

To create happiness, quit wishing or just thinking about what it is you are going to do or be, and get actively involved in your passion pursuit.

SECOND
AXIOM OF HAPPINESS
Believe it to be
Envision and prepare for the future

————◦⟨◉⟩◦————

"If you wish to live a life free from sorrow,
think of what is going to happen
as if it had already happened."
—Epictetus—

Have you ever thought or uttered the phrase, "If I only knew then, what I know now"? The ability to have information from the future and be able to apply it today would produce dramatic differences in our lives. It would be like going back in time armed with powerful knowledge and experience from the future—there would be no stopping us. Those of us with this ability would have an unfair advantage over the rest of the world. We would be living life one step ahead of the game.

The attribute it takes to make "If I only knew then, what I know now" come true is vision. It is imperative that we project ourselves doing or becoming what it is we want to do or become, for vision leads to actions. The actions resulting from vision will propel us towards our intended goals. Belief in ourselves and doing things as if we are already there has the power to transform our vision into reality.

The future imagined comes true
through the efforts of today.

If we are able to foresee ourselves in the future, create a mental image of what it took to get there, bring it back with us, and put the information into use today, the intended goal is well within our grasp. The pursuit of purpose, meaning, and happiness will be enhanced by attempting to fulfill our vision with the efforts of today.

It will be difficult and take a tremendous amount of concentration, sacrifice, and energy on our parts to envision already being where it is we are going. If it were easy, everybody would do it. However, it is absolutely necessary if we are to become what it is we are pursuing. Albert Einstein gave us these memorable words concerning vision: "Imagination is your preview of life's coming attractions."

All of us possess the tremendous capacity to foresee where it is we should be going or what it is we are intended to do. The powerful gift of vision comes from our Creator and enables us to achieve anything we put our minds and hearts to do. If we see our goal—call it destiny, if you like—with clarity and believe that the thing we see in our mind is actually attainable, we can make it so. Imagination, the picturing power of the mind, is an awesome power and provides us with the ability to achieve what we see. As we begin living the dream, our lives will have more purpose, meaning, and happiness, and we will begin experiencing the magnificent aspects of life.

The ability to visualize—seeing and experiencing an event prior to it actually happening—can come with practice. As we pre-experience an event, encounter, or circumstance, we are readying ourselves for that which we desire to happen to actually happen. If we can engage the picturing power of our minds, we can create an air of possibility and opportunity. The process of visualization allows us to take advantage of the possibilities and opportunities that surround us; we are prepared, because the experience has already happened in our minds. As we see ourselves doing that which we have determined is our current mission in life and as we seize opportunities through visualization, our lives will be enriched by the experiences along the way. If we live as if we expect our dreams to come true, they will come true, and dreams that come true add meaning to life.

Envisioning yourself involved in the activities that make you happy will provide you with purpose and direction. Henry David Thoreau gave the world this thought of encouragement: "Go confidently in the directions of your dreams. Live the life you have imagined." Having a purpose and direction motivates each of us to maximize our talents and to reach new heights, which leads us to purposeful happiness.

Let belief and action in dreams
carry you to heights imagined.

Conversely, when an individual is without direction and is willing to settle for less than his or her potential, that person may be on a slippery slope. First, this path may lead to a feeling of being unfulfilled, then bored, then depressed or even destructive to oneself or others. It is important to avoid going through life feeling bitter, miserable, or troubled by a sense of regret that so much was missed; these negative feelings can be avoided by visualizing ourselves in pursuit of our passions. Visualizing oneself in pursuit of a life-long dream or passion fuels the sense of wonder and exuberance for life we all knew as children. Envisioning and preparing for the future will uncover latent abilities and talents which may lie dormant within us, and assist us in becoming supremely happy. As we practice and become proficient at visualizing our goals, we will begin achieving those very goals.

The following poem vividly illustrates the concept of "If I only knew then, what I know now." If we live our life today—right now—with wisdom, vision, and knowledge from the future, then the magnificent experiences of life will be ours to enjoy.

If I Had to Live My Life Over Again

I'd dare to make more mistakes next time.
I'd relax, I would limber up.
I would be sillier than I have been this trip.
I would take fewer things seriously.
I would take more chances.
I would climb more mountains and swim more rivers.
I would eat more ice cream and less beans.
I would perhaps have more actual troubles,
but I'd have fewer imaginary ones.
You see, I'm one of those people who live
sensibly and sanely hour after hour,
day after day.
Oh, I've had my moments,
And if I had it to do over again,
I'd have more of them.
In fact, I'd try to have nothing else.
Just moments, one after another,
instead of living so many years ahead of each day.
I've been one of those people who never goes anywhere
without a thermometer, a hot water bottle, a raincoat
and a parachute.
If I had to do it again, I would travel lighter than I have.
If I had my life to live over,
I would start barefoot earlier in the spring
and stay that way later in the fall.
I would go to more dances.
I would ride more merry-go-rounds.
I would pick more daisies.

—Attributed to Nadine Stair

Visualizing and preparing for the future involves our mind's eye and our thoughts, and results in the ability to control our destiny and our happiness with our perception. The same is true for both the past and the present. What has happened in the past is in the past, and we cannot change it. As for the present, there are a multitude of things over which we have no control. However, there is one thing over which we possess ultimate control—our perception. We have the ability to choose how we interpret the past and the present. It is up to us to find the good, the positive, and to create happiness. The converse is also true; we may choose to see the bad, the negative and to create misery in our lives. We possess the ability to place ourselves in the pursuit of happiness by varying our perspective and seeing the events and circumstances of life in a happy, positive light.

It was a cold December night in West Orange, New Jersey. Thomas Edison's factory was humming with activity. Work was proceeding on a variety of fronts as the great inventor was trying to turn more of his dreams into practical realities. Edison's plant was made of concrete and steel and deemed fireproof. On a frigid night in 1914, this label was proven incorrect; the sky was lit up by a sensational fire that had burst through the plant's roof. Edison's 24-year-old son, Charles, made a frenzied search for his famous inventor/father. When he finally found him, he was watching the fire, his white hair blowing in the wind. His face was illuminated by the leaping flames. Charles thought, "He is 67 years old and everything he has worked for is going up in flames." When Edison saw his son, he shouted, "Charles! Where's your mother?" When Charles responded, "I don't know," he said, "Find her! Bring her here! She'll never see anything like this as long as she lives." The next morning, Mr. Edison looked at the ruins of his factory and said this of his loss: "There's value in disaster. All our mistakes are burned up. Thank God, we can start anew."

What a wonderful perspective on things that seem at first to be so disastrous. Edison chose his perception of the fire to be positive, and the happiness created in his words is almost palpable. This particular event—the fire at the facility—is just an event. It is up to us to interpret the events of our lives.

THE PURSUIT: UP CLOSE AND PERSONAL

Dan, the unfulfilled designer/builder who has uncovered his passion, has visualized himself engaged in an archaeological dig on the Mexican coast. He imagines that he has specialized in the ancient Aztecs and has made a discovery that could lead to the unlocking of the code of the great Aztecan astronomers. He sees himself with students eagerly soaking up this knowledge and the enormity of this event. He has become a teacher, an expert in his field.

Vision uncovers possibility. Possibility combined with determined effort leads to achievement.

While this is currently only happening in his mind, this vision will provide Dan with the necessary motivation during his pursuit. He understands what he has to do to make this vision a reality. He has to go back to school, put in a tremendous amount of time in this field, study under a mentor, and make personal sacrifices. Dan sees himself doing what he has dreamed of doing and sees himself happy doing it as he walks into class with a bunch of twenty-something year-olds.

SECOND AXIOM OF HAPPINESS
BELIEVE IT TO BE... IN A NUTSHELL
To create happiness imagine making "If I only knew then, what I know now" come true. Visualize the future, work at it today.

THIRD
AXIOM OF HAPPINESS
Make time to make it happen
Identify and limit distractions

———•《◉》•———

*"It's the constant and determined effort
that breaks down resistance, sweeps away all obstacles."*
—Claude M. Bristol—

Distractions are obstacles in the path of our passion pursuits. Distractions hinder our progress in becoming what it is we are to be. It is imperative that we first identify distractions, and then limit the impediments to our progress. To create more joy and happiness in life, we need to discover what is robbing us of the limited, precious time we have, and then re-direct that energy to pursuing our passions.

At first it may seem like a simple task to identify distractions, the things slowing us down or holding us back from achieving our goals. However, distractions can be familiar habits, feelings, thoughts, or behaviors to which we have become accustomed. It is difficult to begin a passion pursuit, as well as to stay focused and to devote the necessary time once we have begun. Familiar distractions are easy traps to fall into when we begin to get out of our comfort zone. When we find ourselves in unfamiliar territory or out of control or anxious, it is easy to waste time and try to regain control through these familiar distractions. Familiar distractions are time-wasting bad habits that need to be curtailed, and here are some examples: daydreaming, idle internet use, watching TV, talking on the phone, gambling, feeling sorry for ourselves, arguing, gossiping, blaming, shopping, alcohol/drug abuse, and the list goes on. What is it that is devouring your precious time, taking energy away from achieving your dreams, and keeping you from reaching your potential?

"Is this the way things are supposed to be?" Stephen asks Tabitha. "What do you mean?" she replies. "Look at us, we're living in this trailer, I work at a laundry, we both have college degrees we're not using, and now the baby. How are we ever going to make it?" Tabitha answers with as much conviction as she can muster, "Don't worry, if there's a will, there's a way. We'll make it." "Tabby, I just don't know. I'm going down to The Chug for a beer with the guys," Stephen says as he heads toward the door. "Be careful and don't be too late" came the standard reply she always gave.

As he heads toward the tavern for another night of drinking with his card-playing buddies, his mind wanders between the oppressive laundry that puts food on the table for the young family while simultaneously producing a claustrophobic effect on his creativity, and his dream of being an author, writing books that people want to read. He thinks he has what it takes, but the bats of doubt have begun to take roost in the belfry of his mind. He murmers to himself, "There's always teaching." Right now, though, he is committed to drinking beer, listening to tales describing the conquest of the village's young maidens, and forgetting about the physically and mentally stifling place he has to return to in the morning.

The next evening after supper the same scenario is replayed, except for the fact tonight is card night with the guys. Tabby bids her husband adieu with the well practiced, "Be careful, and don't be too late" as he heads for the card game.

As the cards are shuffled and dealt, beer flows as does the usual banter heard in men's town. Stephen's demeanor is one of preoccupation and is on full display. "Come on Stephen, let's do something before the year's up, it's a quarter to you." "I fold." A question is posed by one of the players, "What's the matter? You look like your dog just got run over." Stephen responds with, "It's just that dead-end job at the laundry.

It's not where I want to be." Another question is presented: "What do you want to do?" "I want to be an author, I want to write books, to be able to tell stories that people want to read." "Yeah, and I want to win a million dollars," and "I want to pitch for the Red Sox" were two of the jabs that were thrown at the aspiring author. On his way home, the taunts reverberated in his mind, and their negativity begins to fuel his transformation.

The next evening during supper, the want-to-be author and supportive wife discuss their situation and dreams. Mutually they agree that Stephen has to continue working at the laundry to provide them with a roof over their heads and food on the table. Stephen reveals honestly without fear of being discouraged, "I want to be a writer, to be able to evoke emotions in people with my words." Tabitha understands the depth of Stephen's passion for writing and suggests, "If you work the eight hours a day we need to pay our bills, I'll take care of everything else, so that you can use your free time to write. What we have to do is make time to make it happen."

Create the time necessary to fulfill dreams.
The effort will be rewarded
with the life which is intended for you.

Stephen puts in the necessary eight hours at the laundry each day while Tabby takes care of everything else required by the young family. They set up a writing workshop in the furnace room of the trailer and Stephen puts aside the distractions and obstacles that have been in the way of his passion of writing and immerses himself in his dream, his destiny. Happiness and joy pour over the author and his family like warm maple syrup over a fresh stack of pancakes.

By changing his attitude, Stephen is able to create more time to devote to his passion. Distractions were leading to discouragement and were trying to gain a foothold in his life. By setting aside the distractions and overcoming discouragement, the transformation from mundane to magnificent was set into motion. The following words of Abraham Lincoln—"Let no feeling of discouragement prey upon you, and in the end you are sure to succeed"—do an excellent job of conveying this meaningful message. By varying his perspective of his situation and eliminating and minimizing the distractions that were robbing him of his precious time, he was able to re-direct that energy to the activity that produced joy and happiness for himself and ultimately his loved ones as well.

Focus, prayer, concentration, or meditation about the distractions in our lives will lead us to an understanding of how they can be overcome. As we identify and then begin to limit the distractions, we will create the time necessary to pursue our vision. The reallocated time which we have created can then be spent on purpose, meaning, and happiness, which allows us to experience the full riches of life.

As our passion pursuit is on the rise, we experience a heightened sense of awareness, and things are seen in a different way. Intuition tells us we are on the right track. Capture these sensations, remember them, and bottle them if possible, for they will be needed along the journey as distractions become obstacles on the path. If we lose focus and take our eyes off the goal, obstacles can instill fear and begin to create doubt. By minimizing distractions, overcoming obstacles, and focusing on our passions, we will continue in the direction of happiness.

*As circumstances of your life change,
passions may wax and wane as do
the phases of the moon.*

Pursuing passions during this waxing (rising) phase is exciting as well as productive, and enthusiasm abounds. Enthusiasm is a tremendous tool when working on a life-defining project and, when properly applied, is capable of producing outstanding results. If we can obtain an enthusiastic, elevated level of effort during our passion pursuits and sustain the effort, we will have discovered one of the key elements necessary to experiencing purposeful happiness. Achievements flourish when enthusiasm is applied to the quest of our dreams.

People viewing the outward results of passion pursuits are often astonished or amazed at the results and wonder how such a life was created. Unless they share an understanding of what it is like to be fulfilling a purpose larger than ourselves, they usually won't grasp the depth of the individual's passion or the level of their commitment required to create what they see. The favorable opinions or approval of others is not our goal. The pursuit of purpose, meaning, and happiness is a personal journey not undertaken to gain the approval of others, and its success or failure is known only in each person's heart.

As life progresses, passions may wane, often due to circumstances beyond our control or to distractions creeping into our lives and robbing us of precious time. The mother whose passion is raising her children, teaching, molding, and helping them develop life skills will see her children grow up and eventually leave home. Her mother's love, commitment, and devotion to her children will not change, but her role changes. To avoid floundering through life without a calling, the empty nest mother will need to discover a new passion toward which she can direct her energy. Beware of ascribing to the stifling belief that our dreams and goals cannot change with time. The journey is full of both change and the possibility for growth, and new challenges await us on the path. We must look upon the pursuit of our desires as an opportunity for discovery about ourselves. It is important that we seek out what life has to offer without fear of failure or disapproval from the people we know. We must guard against limiting or narrowing the possibilities of our purpose, meaning, and happiness in life. Let's shine, look forward, and grow as life moves forward. Helen Keller is credited with giving us these insightful words: "When one door of happiness closes, another opens; but often we look so long at the closed door that we do not see the one which has been opened for us."

Changes in life, increased distractions, or the sense of a diminished passion all may contribute to setting us adrift. To be adrift is to not have a purpose, to not be in control of our destiny, to just go through the motions of life—adrift on the sea of life. People who have no direction have things happen to them not because of them. By not creating their own reality, they are left with accepting what happens to them. The attitude of not being in control creates of sense of "what's the use of trying," and their inability to control their own destiny becomes a self-fulfilling prophecy, since lack of effort produces lack of results. "Adrift" is the condition of having low passions and high distractions— just the opposite of where we should be. If you find yourself in the condition of being adrift, return to Genesis; begin at the beginning by evaluating and identifying passions, then focus, pray, concentrate, or meditate to discover or reinvigorate a worthy purpose.

THE PURSUIT: UP CLOSE AND PERSONAL

Dan, the unfulfilled designer/builder who has uncovered his passion, has made some dramatic changes in his life when it comes to distractions and obstacles that are impeding the fulfillment of his purpose. Dan viewed his job as a distraction to fulfilling his dream of studying ancient civilizations and made the radical decision to become a student in the field of his passion. He chose to make time to make it happen by stepping out of his career, thus creating the time to become a student and eventually an archaeologist and teacher of the ancient ways of life.

THIRD AXIOM OF HAPPINESS
MAKE TIME TO MAKE IT HAPPEN... IN A NUTSHELL

To create happiness, uncover the distractions robbing you of your precious time, limit the distractions, and allocate the new time to your worthy purpose.

FOURTH
AXIOM OF HAPPINESS
Do right, for it is right to do
Evaluate and understand motives

———◦《◉》◦———

*"I know that there is nothing better for men than to be happy
and do good while they live."*
—Ecclesiastes 3:12

In placing oneself in the position to experience purposeful happiness, it is important to evaluate and be cognizant of the reasons for pursing a passion. To be successful in developing a life with purpose, meaning, and happiness, it is essential that our motives have a purity of cause. Pure thoughts and actions assist the growth of our flicker into its intended flame. We must each stay clear of ulterior motives and hidden agendas as well as the temptation to satisfy our shortsighted, selfish ways. It may appear that getting your selfish way by whatever means will make you happy, but appearances can be deceiving. The absence of a pure cause only leads to hollow, false victories. Truth always triumphs. Buddha shed light on this concept with the words "All that we are is the result of what we have thought. If a man speaks or acts with an evil thought, pain follows him. If a man speaks or acts with a pure thought, happiness follows him, like a shadow that never leaves him." We should prepare to experience more joy and happiness in life by pursuing dreams and callings while doing the right things for the right reasons. We must trust our consciences and let them be our guides.

Life is a struggle between selfishness and selflessness. One of the paradoxical battles of our existence is the opposition between our sense of security (selfishness) and our sense of altruism, doing for others (selflessness). Motives which contain a purity of cause and are closer to selfless than selfish will lead us toward transforming our lives from ordinary and mundane to extraordinary and magnificent.

SELFISHNESS   SELFLESSNESS

Enlightenment is gained when there is movement away from selfishness and toward selflessness.

Some may feel a touch of self interest and many believe that "looking out for number one" is necessary to survive in today's ruthless world. This may be practical worldly advice for those who are what they are going to be and have no desire for growth. They are what they are, and nobody is going to take that away from them. We all know people like this who possess a shortsighted, selfish attitude. Are they truly happy? Is it just a coincidence that miser and misery are derived from the same root? If we adopt a selfless attitude, even for a short period of time, the joyful wonders and rewards of this world (the same ruthless world that many believe requires selfishness) will be showered upon us. Happiness will surround us in many unexpected ways. If we can develop the habit of shifting our perspective away from ourselves and towards others, we will find ourselves living a happier, more content life, and we will help raise our collective consciousness to a higher level.

The following commentaries come from an obituary. One doesn't need to have known the individual personally to see the joy and happiness that he must have experienced, likewise for those with whom he came into contact. His selfless attitude served him well in life and created a legacy after his death.

Frank Johnson: Larger than life

His legacy will outlive the stats on the field.

Unselfishness was perhaps what defined Frank Johnson. It wasn't rushing yards or touchdowns, taking his school to bowl games or winning Super Bowl rings. Nor was it money, fame or awards. Nothing defined the Hall of Famer more than the company he kept. And that was never more apparent than last week, when the former football superstar, who died in his sleep Friday night after battling brain cancer, refused to focus on himself in an interview. Instead, he credited good friends and good influence for his success.

... since that time, we've been friends, golf partners, you name it. Frank was a good friend who was as unselfish as the day is long.

... you never knew Frank Johnson played football unless you asked him about it. It wasn't important to him. It was history— just something he did once. He was always more interested in you. He didn't like to talk about himself.

... outside of his family, Johnson dedicated his life to enjoying and creating friendships.

... he didn't want a wake or funeral. He wanted a celebration of life. He wanted people to remember the good times, he wanted his family and friends to sit back, laugh and enjoy a good moment on him.

The actual obituary was quite lengthy and filled with statistics, dates, scores, and other information. However, the theme of the summary of the man's life is quite obvious. The importance of an unselfish attitude which created happiness shines through. How do you want your obituary to read?

Most parents who are actively involved in raising their children, teaching, shaping, and developing them for their own lives, are for the most part doing it for unselfish reasons.

Pure motives combined with passionate effort yield extraordinary results.

The parents are giving of themselves for the good of another; their motives embody this essential purity of cause. They are doing the right thing for the right reason. They are not preparing someone to care for them in their old age. They are giving their children a foundation and the tools necessary to reach their potential. Through their parenting, parents help children in their pursuit of happiness, enabling them to become all that they can be.

Selfishness is capable of producing results. This is evidenced by individuals attaining material possessions, as well as by nations attaining a degree of prosperity. However, selflessness will put an individual, family, or nation onto the pursuit of happiness by making them spiritually rich, economically strong, and socially great.

Once, long ago in the land of the Comanche, there was great drought, famine, and pestilence. The tribes danced to the sound of drums and prayed for rain. They watched and waited, but the healing rains did not come.

Among the children watching the dancers was a small girl named She-Who-Is-Alone. She held closely her warrior doll dressed with beaded leggings and a headdress with brilliant blue feathers from the Jay-Jay bird. She loved the doll very much as it was the only thing she had left from the happy days, the time before the great famine took her parents and grandparents.

As She-Who-is-Alone sat and held her doll, the Wise Man came to speak to the people. He told them that the Great Spirits were unhappy. He said that the people had been selfish, taking everything from the earth and giving nothing in return. He said that the people must make a sacrifice and must make a burnt offering of their most prized possession. The Wise Man said the ashes of this offering should be scattered to the home of the Four Winds: North, South, East, and West. When this sacrifice was made, the drought would cease. Life would be restored to the land.

The people talked among themselves. The warriors were sure it was not their bow that the Great Spirits wanted. The women knew that is was not their special blanket. She-Who-Is-Alone looked at her doll, her most valued possession, knew what the Great Spirits wanted, and knew what she must do.

While everyone slept, she took her warrior doll and one stick from the teepee fire and went to the hill where the Wise Man had spoken. "Oh Great Spirits," she called out, "here is my warrior doll, the only thing I have from the happy days with my family. It is my most valued possession. Please accept it."

She made a fire and thrust her precious doll into it. When the flames died down, she scooped up a handful of ashes and scattered them to the Four Winds: North, South, East, and West. As she went to sleep that night, her cheeks were wet from tears.

The first light of morning woke her, and she looked out over the hills. Covering the hills where the ashes had fallen were flowers, beautiful blue flowers, as blue as the feathers in her beloved doll's hair. Now every spring the Great Spirits remember the sacrifice of a very small girl and fill the hills and valleys of the land of the Comanche with beautiful blue flowers.

The legend passed down by the Comanche illustrates the importance of moving away from selfish and toward selfless. Because the important axiom needed to be passed onto future generations the legend was created. The higher state of enlightenment and selflessness, personified in the actions of the little girl, are splendidly contrasted against small-minded, selfish actions of the elder members of the tribe. Moving toward selfless thoughts and actions and gaining enlightenment will facilitate your transformation from mundane to magnificent.

In addition to bringing our motives closer to selfless than selfish, our attempts to fulfill our dreams should serve as an inspiration, as an example to others of the possibilities of the human spirit. We have been given a great gift. We should treat our lives as such. What does one do when given a great gift? Do they keep it to themselves, locked up and hidden away, like a miser? Or, do they put it on display to exhibit the beauty of the gift and demonstrate its magnitude?

We all have great gifts waiting to be displayed. The gifts and the level of talents that are attached to our gifts are as varied, diverse, and unique as each one of us. We are all not designed to be world renowned artists creating works of art to stimulate the senses. A person's gift may be courage and faith displayed in the face of a terminal illness. A gift such as this may affect and inspire both caregivers and loved ones, in addition to producing substantial changes in the lives of those who witnessed the gift in action. As our gifts, whatever they may be, are demonstrated and become examples of the possibilities of the human spirit, the riches of life will be delivered to us. As we become a shining beacon, a trailblazer that shows how to do the right things for the right reasons, not only will we be on the path to supreme happiness, we will inspire others to see the light.

THE PURSUIT: UP CLOSE AND PERSONAL

Dan, the unfulfilled designer/builder who has uncovered his passion, reached over and turned the blaring alarm clock off. It was a cold, blustery winter morning—the type of day on which it is easy to pull the covers over your head and sleep an extra hour. Dan rolled out of bed and got ready to head to the gym. Since starting the exercise routine, he has enjoyed his time in the gym, and it has made him feel better. The early morning workout was his private time reserved for himself.

On the drive to the gym, he drove past a limping woman and a bundled up child walking on the snow-covered sidewalk. As he drove past, he thought, "Someone ought to... No, I'll be late for my workout and then late for work." One block down the road, his selfish thoughts were vanquished by his conscience, and he turned around.

During the drive to the school, Dan found out that Nala walked Martha to school everyday so Martha could receive additional English lessons before school. The mother and daughter were recent immigrants to the United States from Liberia. Learning of their plight, Dan decided to do the right thing and alter his daily exercise routine to include transportation for the mother and daughter.

His thoughts and actions inspired by the needs of someone besides himself created a spiritual awakening. Dan began to deeply examine his life and, as a result, he became aware of the selfish tendencies that were prevalent in it. The realization energized Dan to try and serve other's needs ahead of his own. The families of Dan and Nala became friends, and Dan's action—doing right, for it is right to do—created much happiness in many lives. Good deeds and thoughts will be reflected back to us as will the negative ones. Create more joy and happiness in life by doing right, for it will be returned to you like a reflection in a mirror.

The mirror of life cannot be deceived.
Our thoughts and actions, both good and bad,
will be reflected back onto us.

The good we see in others is in us as well. The faults we find in others are faults which reside within us. To understand and recognize something, we must know it. The possibilities that exist in others are possible for us. Beauty surrounds us, and it's up to us to see that which is beautiful. The world in which we live is a reflection of us, a mirror showing us who we are. To change our world, we must change ourselves. Blaming and complaining that the world won't make us happy only makes matters worse. We are responsible and accountable for ourselves in thoughts and actions. See the best in others, and we will be our best. Give to others, and we give to ourselves. Appreciate beauty, and we will be beautiful. Admire creativity, and we will be creative. Love, and we will be loved. Seek to understand, and we will be understood. Listen, and our voices will be heard. Teach, and we will learn.

If your heart desires happiness, fulfillment, or inner peace, the words of Psalm 37:3–4 give some direction toward those goals: "³Trust in the Lord and do good; dwell in the land and enjoy safe pasture. ⁴Delight yourself in the Lord and he will give you the desires of your heart." Be assured and confident that doing the right thing for the right reason will produce the goals you desire.

My purpose in writing this book is to help people live with purpose, meaning, and happiness. The Nine Axioms of Happiness are intended to help people realize dreams, transform their lives from mundane to magnificent, and to give thanks to our Creator for our blessings.

FOURTH AXIOM OF HAPPINESS
DO RIGHT, FOR IT IS RIGHT TO DO... IN A NUTSHELL
To create happiness, do the right things for the right reasons. Move away from selfishness and toward selflessness.

FIFTH
AXIOM OF HAPPINESS
Receive inspiration, provide motivation
Associate with fellow passion seekers

"Pay any price to stay in the presence of extraordinary people."
—Mike Murdock—

As geese migrate south to warmer climates for the winter and eventually return north in the spring, it is not a coincidence that they fly together in a "V" formation with their distinctive honking. The geese fly in a "V" because as each goose flaps its wings, it creates uplift for the birds that follow, and the effect of flying as a flock adds 71% greater flying range than if each bird were to fly alone. When a goose falls out of formation, it suddenly feels the drag and resistance of flying alone and, as a result, quickly moves back into formation, taking advantage of the lifting power generated by the bird in front of it. The geese from behind lend their assistance by honking to encourage the ones in front of them.

Travel with passion seekers,
for during the voyage the ways to purpose,
meaning, and happiness will be revealed

Mother Nature provides us with an important lesson in the way the geese work together to get where they are going. The same lesson is pertinent for us. If we want a happy, successful life, then we should surround ourselves with people who are going where we want to go. We must seek out and learn from people who possess an aura of happiness and contentment, who are living life on their terms, and who seem to radiate happiness and joy. Like the geese flying in formation, we will reach our goals when traveling with people who have a similar goal. Receive inspiration—the metaphorical uplift created by the person in front of you—and provide motivation—the honking encouragement from behind. Remember, each goose is constantly inspiring and motivating a fellow traveler either in front of or behind itself. This is done by each individual so that all involved can reach the goal.

When growing up, parents tell their kids they don't want them hanging out with certain other kids. These are the kids who drink and smoke, and who are inconsiderate, lazy, and headed for trouble. Why is this? It's because parents know that who we hang out with is who we are likely to become. The same is true in a positive way; if we are going to be happy and successful, then we must associate with happy, successful people. We need to ask these people how they were able to get where they are. It is helpful to try to implement what works for them, by thinking like they think, acting like they act, and reading what they read. Jim Rohn put it this way: "You are the average of the five people you spend the most time with." Due to our unique abilities and ways of doing things, each individual will not eventually adopt everything he or she tries. Instead, we must each keep plugging away. This tenacity will soon lead each of us to develop our own success formula for turning our flickering lights into blazing flames.

Becoming friends, acquaintances, or associates of people who we determine to possess insight and enlightenment in regards to living a life with joy will place us in a position to receive inspiration. Coach

Vince Lombardi, one of the greatest football coaches ever, said "Confidence is contagious. So is lack of confidence." The same can be said of happiness and unhappiness, which is why we want to surround ourselves with good, supportive people and to avoid people with poisonous, negative personalities. We need to steer clear of people who attempt to hold us back, who possess a victim mentality, or who want to bring us down to their level. Instead, it is important to seek out passion seekers, those people who follow their dreams, for they have enlightenment that will provide us with inspiration.

Our association with fellow passion seekers is not a one-way street; instead, inspiration flows in both directions. The relationship is mutually beneficial relationship for all parties involved and is characterized by a balance of give and take. In this way, we resemble the geese: flying in the "V" formation, receiving inspiration, and providing motivation. As we receive inspiration, it is our duty to turn our flickers to flames so that the people who inspired us may see our bright flames and, in turn, be inspired and motivated. Also, we must be prepared to assist others who seek answers as they recognize the flame. "It is one of the most beautiful compensations of this life that no man can sincerely try to help another without helping himself," are the words of Ralph Waldo Emerson.

THE PURSUIT: UP CLOSE AND PERSONAL

Dan, the unfulfilled designer/builder who has uncovered his passion, has created happiness in his life by joining a mastermind group. The mastermind group is made up of six people from all different walks of life who meet monthly for the purpose of encouraging, motivating, inspiring, solving problems, and brainstorming with each other. The group brings to the members new ideas, knowledge, resources, and spiritual energy. They are able to harness the power that comes from each of the participants, as well as the power that comes from our Creator.

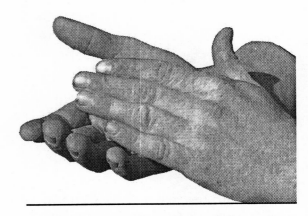

Providing motivation and inspiration
has a reciprocal effect.
As it is given, it will also be received.

Each month when they meet, they follow the same guidelines. They begin by asking for spiritual guidance. They then share what's good and new, and set time guidelines for the meeting. The individuals then take turns speaking while the group listens and brainstorms, they make commitments to accomplish something before the next meeting, and they end with a moment of thanks. Dan has surrounded himself, as have the other members of the group, with good, supportive people, and he feels happiness growing as he receives inspiration and provides motivation.

FIFTH AXIOM OF HAPPINESS
RECEIVE INSPIRATION, PROVIDE MOTIVATION... IN A NUTSHELL
To create happiness, surround yourself with happy, successful people. Learn from others and become an example.

SIXTH
AXIOM OF HAPPINESS
Pass it on
Teach others and express gratitude

———— ◉ ————

*"We cannot hold a torch to light another's path
without brightening our own."*
—Ben Sweetland—

The ship was lost at sea. There was wind to power the sails, but the young captain did not know which direction they were headed. For many days the overcast sky and fog had blocked their only tool for orienting themselves, the sun. The captain knew they wanted to go in the direction of the setting sun, because it was rumored that in that direction there were traders with exquisite treasures for which he could trade his cargo. But, which way was it? The young captain and crew grew anxious. Would they be able to find their way? What unknown perils were waiting? Sailing blind was becoming dangerous.

"Ship ahoy" came the cry from the look-out. A ship with strange black and gold markings, with which the young captain was unfamiliar, was approaching extremely close to the lost ship. Neither ship displayed any hostile intentions. The two vessels passed close enough for the young captain of the lost ship to yell out, "Do you know the direction of the setting sun?" A response came back from the mysterious black and gold ship asking if they were lost and needed help.

Assisting others during the voyage of life adds purpose, meaning, and happiness to the journey.

The captains met. The captain of the black and gold ship asked the young captain "You asked if we knew the direction of the setting sun, are you lost?" The young captain replied "Yes, we haven't seen the sun for many days and we're not sure of our direction. Are you not lost as well?" "I don't use the sun as our guide. I use a direction device which always tells me which direction we are traveling." The captain of the black and gold ship proceeds to tell the young captain in great detail how to find the magnetic lodestone and how to attach the needle so it points north. He gives him detailed instructions so that the young captain may construct his own device. He also retrieves his own ship's extra direction device and gives it to the young captain.

*Generous actions point both giver and receiver
in the direction of happiness.*

The young captain was overwhelmed by his counterpart's generosity in offering such a valuable gift. "Thank you, I'll remember this day for as long as I live. I'm curious, how did you learn of the direction device?" The captain of the black and gold ship responds with his own tale of being lost at sea because he could not see the sun, just like the young captain and his crew. He further describes his encounter with Master Coompa, and how the Master taught him how to use and build the direction device. The young captain asked, "Do you ever see Master Coompa?" "Our paths cross occasionally, and whenever I see him, I always express my gratitude for what he taught me and tell him stories about people like you." The young captain promises, "I'll never forget what you have taught me, and I'll be sure to pass it on." As the two men rose to part ways, the captain of the black and gold ship said, "That's the way it's meant to be."

Teaching assisting, or inspiring someone who has a purpose or calling similar to yours produces happiness in a variety of ways. Observing the student or associate absorbing and utilizing the knowledge provided or taking the inspiration in new, different directions will produce satisfaction and happiness. The art of passing it on comes with the added benefit of simultaneously renewing your passion. Joy and exuberance is also created in the life of the student or associate who has received the assistance or inspiration. The amount of happiness created during the exchange when the captain of the black and gold ship teaches the young captain how to use and construct Coompa's direction device is palpable. The young captain is overjoyed by the wonderful gift of knowledge that will change his life. He is happy because of what it means to him specifically and, more generally, because of how it reinforces to him the way happiness can be transmitted to others by teaching. This general source of happiness constitutes another valuable gift or lesson he has received as a result of their conversation. The captain, who passed along the device, experiences happiness by being of assistance to another and seeing the joy it has created. When he relays the tale of passing along what he has received to Master Coompa, happiness will be enjoyed again by both men. These reoccurring acts of teaching and expressing gratitude may go on indefinitely, thus producing happiness in the lives of people they touch. When the joyful life circle of teaching and thanking appears in your life, pass it on!

Teaching, assisting, or inspiring others is a necessary element to place both teacher and student in the pursuit of happiness. To create happiness in each of our lives as well as in the life of another, we must assist those that we come in contact with to become what they are capable of becoming. Johann Wolfgang von Goethe wrote these inspiring words: "Treat people as if they were what they ought to be, and you help them to become what they are capable of being." By teaching and helping place another on the path toward the fulfillment of his or her destiny, we will have helped admit another to the culture of happiness and joy. We will also have helped create a passion seeker, another supportive soul as described in the Fifth Axiom: Receive inspiration, provide motivation: Associate with fellow passion seekers.

Teaching, coupled with the expression of gratitude that follows, produces happiness. The communication and exchange of information between motivated teacher and eager student creates a bond that produces an immediate joyous effect. This interaction when relived in the minds of both teacher and student will create happiness again. Heartfelt gratitude is an elevated state of gratitude that is characterized by feelings of true appreciation. "To appreciate" means to express approval and admiration, enjoyment and pleasure. Appreciation also implies a sense of understanding, acceptance, and responsiveness. Heartfelt gratitude, deep true appreciation, is the place where miracles happen. It creates joy for both the giver and the receiver, and it breaks down the barriers of resistance that keep us from creating lives of true fulfillment. "Gratitude unlocks the fullness of life. It turns what we have into enough, and more. It turns denial into acceptance, chaos to order, confusion to clarity. It can turn a meal into a feast, a house into a home, a stranger into a friend. Gratitude makes sense of our past, brings peace for today, and creates a vision for tomorrow," are the words of Melody Beattie. The best thing about heartfelt gratitude is that the more you practice it, the more it grows. And the more it grows, the more valuable you feel and the more valuable you become to yourself and to others. What we focus on grows. The more we focus on what we appreciate, the more we'll have to appreciate.

THE PURSUIT: UP CLOSE AND PERSONAL

Dan, the unfulfilled designer/builder who has uncovered his passion, contacts his professor from college, the one who led the first dig he participated in. Dan informs the professor of his decision to go back to college to become an archaeologist and teacher. Dan also thanks him for initially sparking his interest in the history of ancient civilizations. The professor asks Dan to stay in touch and to keep him informed of his progress. The exchange between the two men leaves them both with a feeling of joy.

Later that evening, Dan's four-year son asks him, "Daddy tie my shoe." Dan replies, "How about if we try together and I'll show you how to tie it?" "Okay, Daddy." The father and son work together tying, untying, and then re-tying the boy's shoe. After awhile, the boy says, "Daddy, let me do it. I think I can do it. Cross 'em, pull it tight, make a loop, go 'round the loop, poke it through, pull 'em tight. I did it! I did it! Daddy, I'm a big boy now." "You certainly are son, I'm proud of you." The exchange between father and son—teacher and student—created much happiness in two lives.

Approaching any subject with the consciousness that you are responsible for teaching the subject matter to someone causes you to focus, concentrate, and assimilate the subject thoroughly. The responsibility of teaching results in thorough comprehension of the subject which, in turn, creates a deeper understanding. In our case, the result is a deeper understanding of the Nine Axioms of Happiness. If you desire happiness in your life, learn and put into practice the nine axioms and teach those around you the necessary elements to create happiness. There is one thing greater than experiencing happiness, and that is to help someone else to experience happiness. Learn the nine axioms with the idea that you are going to teach them to others. Not only will you create more joy and happiness in your life through better understanding of the axioms, but you will also have helped another person close to you experience more happiness in his or her life. Your knowledge and understanding as it is passed along will be absorbed, refined, and disseminated by others, and ultimately we all benefit as humanity progresses toward a more divine-like state.

In order for the Nine Axioms of Happiness to produce results, they must be incorporated into daily life. They must become habits, a way of life. Teaching the axioms will keep you on the path of learning and enlightenment because when you teach, you learn again. Use this book as your reference guide to happiness and teach others the way to be happy. You will find yourself creating the life you have envisioned.

SIXTH AXIOM OF HAPPINESS
PASS IT ON... IN A NUTSHELL

To create happiness, share knowledge and resources and thank those who shared with you. Help others to be happy by teaching the Nine Axioms of Happiness.

SEVENTH
AXIOM OF HAPPINESS
Experience joy
Recognize and receive rewards

———◦((◦))◦———

"Joy is the holy fire that keeps our purpose warm
and our intelligence aglow."
—Helen Keller—

Following our callings, exhibiting our talents, pursuing passions, or engaging in activities for which we have an affinity will prepare us to receive the Four Experiences of Profound Joy: epiphany, omni, golden moment, and reflection. These deeply joyful experiences are unique and special gifts that when received should be appreciated and enjoyed. Our existence will be enhanced when we prepare ourselves to receive the Four Experiences of Profound Joy. To ready ourselves we must first be aware. We must have an understanding of the four concepts so that we may appreciate the experiences when they occur. Second, we must be engaged in a purpose we consider or deem worthy to create these wonderful experiences. The experiences of epiphany, omni, golden moment, and reflection, when not linked to a worthy purpose, will not produce Profound Joy. Instead, they will provide for the enjoyable experience of momentary happiness. The resulting momentary happiness, while enjoyable, pales in comparison to the Profound Joy an individual receives when these experiences occur while fulfilling a purpose. To truly appreciate the special gifts of Profound Joy, we must understand their meaning and importance and be ready to receive them by participating in a meaningful purpose. With awareness and passion participation as a foundation, some of these experiences of Profound Joy may be so powerful that they will be carried with us throughout our lives. When panning for gold, one must understand the properties of gold before getting into the stream. It is useless to pan for gold on city streets.

EPIPHANY

For our purpose, epiphany is a flash of insight or the experience that brings this about. If you are fortunate enough to experience an epiphany while engaged in your worthy purpose, it has the potential to be a deeply moving, motivating, and memorable experience. Crystal clear acuity, razor sharp wisdom, and acute enlightenment are some of the characteristics of an epiphany that occurs while fulfilling your purpose. This experience can be motivating, life altering, and capable of producing profoundly joyous moments in your life, both while it is occurring and as it is relived. I was fortunate enough to personally experience a powerful epiphany while engaged in an emerging purpose. As a matter of fact, it was that epiphany which is responsible for the creation of this book.

My wife and I were in the Bahamas for a meeting at The Westin at Our Lucaya Beach and Golf Resort, Lucaya Grand Bahamas Island and, after a morning presentation, we had a free afternoon to enjoy. My wife headed poolside to sunbathe and read. As I'm not a sunbather, I decided to hang out in the room and relax. As I was lying on the bed in the peaceful tropical setting, my mind was clear and free of distractions; it was at this moment that the epiphany struck me.

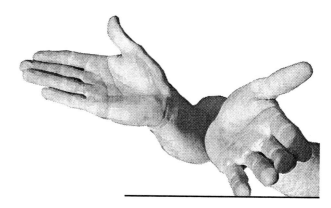

When the light of discovery
reveals an ultimate calling,
destiny is set in motion.

My mind was flooded, filled with ideas and thoughts about how we are all given a gift—a light—by our Creator, and that by discovering our gifts and letting our light shine, we allow ourselves to live a life with joy and happiness. I grabbed a pen and paper and just started writing to collect the thoughts that were cascading out of my mind, through my hand, and onto the paper. I was writing on every piece of paper I could find. Hours went by like minutes, minutes like seconds, and after three hours of real time had passed, I walked down to the pool and told my wife, "I just wrote my book." It wasn't the actual complete form you are reading here, but it was the genesis for the book. Needless to say, she was a little surprised.

My wife and I have been married going on twenty years, and she knew that someday I would write a book because I kept telling her I had a book inside me. Personally, I've known it for longer than that. Prior to writing this book, the only thing I have ever had published, if you can call it that, was my mom's obituary, which I wrote four months prior to the epiphany. Included with the obituary was the following tribute which appeared in our local newspaper. Besides being mom, a business partner, and friend, she was an inspiration. She passed away at the young age of 67 after a courageous four year battle with breast cancer.

JUANITA... A TRIBUTE TO A SPECIAL PERSON

Her gift was her ability to inspire. She has left a lasting impression on all of us who called her Juanita, Mom, Grandma, or Mrs. Parker. She inspired all of us with her love, hope, faith, kindness, and courage.

LOVE
Her love, devotion, and dedication to her family were endless. Her love has and will continue to inspire us.

HOPE
Her hope that everything will work out for the best will always be remembered. Her hope has and will continue to inspire us.

FAITH
Her faith in God, and Jesus as her personal savior, has given her rest with eternal peace. Her faith has and will continue to inspire us.

KINDNESS
Her kindness, which was a way of life for her, was rewarded with the large number of people who called her "friend." Her kindness has and will continue to inspire us.

COURAGE
Her courage to face any obstacles life put in front of her with her quiet resolve was inspirational. Her courage has and will continue to inspire us.

THOUGHTS OF A LOVING SON
"What you leave behind is not what is engraved in stone monuments, but what is woven into the lives of others."
—Pericles, ancient Greek politician and general, 495–429 BC

Back to the epiphany in the Bahamas—a few minutes after the revelation to my wife concerning the book I had just written about living a life with happiness, we headed to the gift shop. There, next to the cash register, was a magazine rack with a prominently displayed Time magazine. On the cover was a large, yellow smiley face and the title "The Science of Happiness." Clearly, this was a message or a very strange coincidence. Of course, I bought the magazine, and I still have it.

The motivation and inspiration I received that day stayed with me during the next year while I wrote this book. I have no doubt that my epiphany in the Bahamas will continue to create happiness for me throughout my life.

epiphany + worthy purpose = Experience of Profound Joy

OMNI

Omni is the Latin prefix for all and in the context of the Four Experiences of Profound Joy, omni denotes when everything seems to be going right. Omni describes a condition of complete self-realization. As we experience omni, we fulfill our potential and everything seems to come together—difficult tasks are completed with ease and the importance of time is lost as we become deeply focused on the task at hand. Omni allows us to create a sense that anything is possible and all is right in the universe. Omni has an equivalent in the sporting world: being in the zone. A golfer who hits long drives in the middle of the fairway, followed up with shots that are chipped in, and forty foot putts that confidently find the hole, experiences omni.

Omni, like all of the Four Experiences of Profound Joy, needs to be understood and linked with involvement in your worthy purpose. Otherwise, it will only produce momentary happiness.

Susan had been working for days on preparing her personal income taxes. The tedious task was a struggle, filled with locating receipts, reading about deductions, and trying to understand the changes in the new tax code. Then, like a light coming on in her head, she got it. What seemed difficult became understandable, and the whole process seemed to flow. It was as if all things came together and she completed her goal of preparing her income taxes. The experience produces momentary happiness, a temporary euphoric feeling in her life.

The next day, she returns home from her job as a pharmaceutical sales rep. With her mind now clear of tax preparation thoughts, she heads to her studio. An idea for her next painting, the one she knew was residing somewhere within her, finally reveals itself. As the paints are being artfully applied to the canvas, the concept of time becomes lost to Susan. She is so highly focused on her worthy purpose—her passion of painting—that she is transported to a place that she has not known before. Time seems to stand still and she stops thinking and is just doing. She is experiencing a sense of all—not awe, but *all*—in the sense that all is right.

The emergence and subsequent realization of a dream leads to profound joy.

Susan finally puts the brush down in the wee hours of the morning; she has to get some sleep as she has work in the morning. While getting ready for bed, Susan is aware and appreciative of what she just experienced.

Susan experienced omni in two varying degrees. The first experience of omni, getting her taxes done, only produced momentary happiness, as it was void of her worthy purpose. For the second omni experience, both omni and her worthy purpose were in line, which produced an Experience of Profound Joy. All seemed right, the paint flowed onto the canvas, and time seemed to stand still. This Profound Joy was different from momentary happiness because it contained the component of a worthy purpose. The painting experience will continue to produce happiness and joy long after the feeling of momentary happiness, produced by finishing her taxes, is forgotten.

omni + worthy purpose = Experience of Profound Joy

GOLDEN MOMENT

An unexpected event that produces a joyous effect is the definition of a golden moment. The golden moment may produce momentary happiness or, as mentioned earlier, if linked to a worthy purpose, it may result in an Experience of Profound Joy. A golden moment experienced while engaged in fulfilling our purpose or pursuing our passions may provide us with an unforgettable experience, take our breath away in amazement, or almost leave us speechless. The combination of a worthy purpose and a golden moment will produce a lifetime of joyous thoughts as the moment is remembered, retold, and relived.

Warm tropical breezes blowing in gently off the Pacific, waves caressing the sandy beach with a soothing melody, warm welcome sunshine while partaking of a spicy Mexican lunch beachside at the Westin Hotel in Puerto Vallarta was the idyllic setting for the genesis of an exciting golden moment. My wife and I were attending a conference where Jay Conrad Levinson was the keynote speaker. We were excited to hear a talk given by Levinson, who is the author of "Guerilla Marketing" and numerous other books which have sold millions worldwide, who helped create the Marlboro Man and the Pillsbury Doughboy, and who has literally changed the way the world does business. After the informative, inspirational words presented by Mr. Levinson, it was time for a break and the beachside lunch.

After lunch, my wife and I approached Mr. Levinson and his wife and thanked him for his words of wisdom. During our conversation, I mentioned I was in the process of writing a book, and he inquired about the subject. We further discussed the writing and publishing of books, and I asked him if he could possibly read my nearly finished manuscript, which I had back in my room, and give me some feedback. He agreed to do so, as he said he had a few free days in Puerto Vallarta.

Golden moments are the unexpected joys
encountered during a passion pursuit.

The next day at 5:15 pm, the golden moment that produced an Experience of Profound Joy struck. Jay Levinson called my room and said, "Jeff?" I responded with "Yes." He said, "This is Jay, I just finished you book. This book must be published, the world needs this message. I just finished reading it out loud with my wife. What a wonderful experience reading it here in this tropical setting. Thank you for letting me read it." He went on with other complimentary comments before we concluded the conservation by exchanging contact information. I thanked him, of course, for his time and his kind words, though I was on the verge of being speechless.

This unexpected affirmation of my manuscript by a renowned author and marketing icon such as Jay Conrad Levinson was a golden moment that produced an Experience of Profound Joy. This golden moment resulted in Profound Joy only because it was linked to my worthy purpose of writing a book to help others transform their existence into one with meaning and purposeful happiness. I feel extremely fortunate to have had the opportunity to have this experience and continue to give thanks for its occurrence. It is an experience I will carry with me throughout my life.

Be aware of the concept of golden moment while engaged in your worthy purpose, so that you may receive and appreciate the experience as it occurs. Enjoy and give thanks when a golden moment appears in your life.

golden moment + worthy purpose = Experience of Profound Joy

REFLECTION (SENSE OF ACCOMPLISHMENT)

The sense of accomplishment that is felt when finishing a task, the sigh you take when looking back at the completed handiwork is known as reflection. When reflection is combined with the ongoing fulfillment of a worthy purpose, the fourth Experience of Profound Joy is the result. Reflection without the simultaneous pursuit of a passion (events such as mowing the yard, cleaning the house in preparation for guests, or closing a deal at work), may still produce that sense-of-accomplishment sigh, but the result will be momentary happiness, because a worthy purpose is lacking.

Reflecting on a job well done,
especially one deemed to be a worthy purpose
gives meaning to life.

"Not everyone aspires to be a bank president or a nuclear scientist, but everybody wants to do something with one's life that will give him pride and a sense of accomplishment," are the words of the 40th President of the United States, Ronald Reagan. The implied meaning of the quote is what I have attempted to express in the title of this book: Everybody wants a chance to fulfill their purpose, to transform their flicker to flame. The words "do something with one's life" could very well be substituted with "have a worthy purpose." This book was written after his death, but it is clear President Reagan understood the concept of the fourth Experience of Profound Joy.

Carol, the director of the local Habitat for Humanity chapter, was helping to put the finishing touches on the latest Habitat for Humanity house, a project at 636 N. Adams Street. Tomorrow would be the day that the keys would be presented to the Martinez family. Carol's worthy purpose is heading up the local chapter that builds affordable homes for people in need.

During the presentation ceremony, Roberto and Inez Martinez thanked and hugged all the volunteers who helped make their dream of home ownership come true. Carol, after receiving the heartfelt gratitude of Roberto and Inez, took a moment to reflect on what she helped to accomplish. As the excited and grateful couple crossed the threshold of their dream, Carol looked back upon her contribution to the house as well as upon her job as director and thought, "This is good." Carol was able to have an Experience of Profound Joy as reflection was linked to her worthy purpose.

reflection + worthy purpose = Experience of Profound Joy

SEVENTH AXIOM OF HAPPINESS
EXPERIENCE JOY... IN A NUTSHELL

To create happiness, first be aware of joyful experiences, then receive and appreciate them as they occur.

EIGHTH
AXIOM OF HAPPINESS
The tree of three
Nurture body, mind, and spirit

———————⊨⊲◍⊳⊨———————

"Body and mind, and spirit
all combine to make the Creature, human and divine."
—Ella Wheeler Wilcox—

Trees. They are brilliantly complex yet simple, beautiful, and necessary, and they silently perform an integral part in sustaining life on this planet. Trees produce oxygen, absorb carbon dioxide, provide food and shelter, protect from erosion, help produce fertile soil by providing fallen leaves which decay, provide shade for cooling, and are aesthetically pleasing with their majestic canopies and magnificent array of colors in autumn.

A tree basically consists of roots, a trunk, and leaves. The roots absorb water and nutrients from the soil which are transported through the trunk to the leaves. As the leaves obtain the water and nutrients, they manufacture food with the help of energy from the sun, a process known as photosynthesis. This food is then transported through the trunk to the roots and other parts of the tree for growth. If the roots are not healthy or are damaged, the tree will not grow. If the water is tainted or if the nutrients the roots absorb are not good, this also inhibits growth. If the trunk is hollow or has decay, the tree will not reach its potential. If the leaves don't properly absorb the sun's life-giving light, the tree will not grow.

Remember, what the roots are to a tree, the body is to an individual's happiness; they both need to be healthy and active and both are vital, the first for the tree's growth and the second for our happiness. The trunk, like the spirit, serves as a conduit; in both cases, the medium must not be hollow while, at the same time, it must be free of decay. Both conduits are vital, the first to the tree's growth and the second to our happiness. The leaves function in a similar way to the mind; both are constantly absorbing, the one sunlight and the other knowledge, and in doing so, leaves are vital to a tree's growth, whereas the mind is essential to our happiness.

The essence of human existence is three interwoven aspects: the triad of body, mind, and spirit. An important component in the transformation of our flicker, which will elevate our lives to a higher state that has purpose, meaning, and happiness, is the nurturing of body, mind, and spirit. These three distinctively different yet linked elements of our lives need continual care and attention. If neglected, a downward spiral into the abysmal existence of mediocrity can be expected. On the positive side, promoting the development and improvement of body, mind, and spirit will lead to energy, knowledge, and enlightenment, which will help us in the pursuit of happiness.

BODY

Our body is truly a remarkable gift. Its design and function is an unsurpassed, unique marvel. We need to treat our bodies like the wonderful gifts they are. Caring for our bodies through proper nutrition, exercise, and sufficient rest and relaxation will provide energy which, when applied to our passions, will lead to purposeful happiness.

Body, mind, and spirit, which constitute the essence of our existence, are interconnected and if one area is neglected, the other two will also suffer. "To keep the body in good health is a duty, otherwise we shall not be able to keep our mind strong and clear," are the words of Buddha. These words exemplify the timeless truth of the concept. Awareness of the importance of nurturing our bodies as well as the specific actions that this nurturing requires (nutrition, exercise, and rest and relaxation) will have a positive effect on our minds and spirits and will allow our flames to burn bright.

If a horse were the only means of transportation, we would look after it with much care and attention because if we didn't, we would be stranded. The horse would provide us with freedom to travel as we pleased and to do the things we needed or were supposed to do. It would be important to us that the horse be properly fed and have enough water to drink. We would make sure the horse was strong enough to carry us and our provisions. We would not take out an untested or unreliable horse on an important journey. Finally, we would give the horse the proper rest so it would be prepared for the next day's ride. The horse, like our bodies, needs the proper care to take us where we are going.

To be transported to the life intended,
proper care of the body is required.

In order for us to transform our lives or to realize our dreams, we have to feel good. This involves feeling good about ourselves in general, but also feeling well physically. Our health and wellness can't ever be isolated from our pursuit of purpose, meaning, and happiness. Our nutritional habits have a vital role in allowing us to live the lives we have envisioned. Some of the basic, common sense guidelines to good nutritional habits include (a) avoid missing meals, (b) drink plenty of water, (c) eat five fruits and vegetables a day, and (d) choose lean cuts of meat. Good eating habits should be learned and incorporated in order to properly fuel our bodies. By increasing our knowledge of sound nutritional information and putting into practice a healthy lifestyle, the body, mind, and spirit will benefit and further advance our progression toward the life we are intended to live.

Exercising our body is another extremely important aspect in our overall health and well-being. A good exercise program consists of building our body in strength, flexibility, and endurance. Our unique qualities—which we bring to life—dictate that each of us will approach the topic of exercise in a different manner. It is necessary to read, watch, listen, and expand the mind with learning about exercise and to apply the information, as each of us strives to become in tune with our bodies. To improve our bodies through a habit of regular, strenuous exercise will produce more energy to be devoted to our individual worthy purposes.

Rest and relaxation are the final elements to caring for our bodies. We all require rest daily to recharge our batteries. Some can get by on less sleep than others, though it imperative that we understand and receive the proper amount of restful sleep required by each of us. Is there anything more important in life than relaxation? In order for us to experience joy and live life to its fullest extent, we have to free ourselves of the tension and stress that are a part of everyday life. It's an undeniable truth that physical health and spiritual growth are enhanced by simple relaxation. As we seek and practice what truly relaxes us, we will find that our pursuit of purpose, meaning, and happiness is profoundly more enjoyable. Ella Wheeler Wilcox, a 19th century American poet, started her poem "Solitude" with, "Laugh, and the world laughs with you. Weep and you weep alone." The same thing could be said about relaxation. Relax, and the world relaxes with you. Forego relaxation, become stressed out and exhausted, and you'll find yourself isolated.

MIND

Our minds have awesome and incredible powers that are capable of taking us where it is we want to go. If we succeed in harnessing the powerful resource that is our minds, we will be presented with the chance to discover and experience the wonderful joys intended for us. Exercising and expanding our minds lead to understanding and prepare us to seize opportunities presented to us in the activities we have deemed worthy purposes. Thus, as our worthy purposes grow with enlightenment and opportunity, the amount of joy we experience also grows. As we utilize our minds to learn, to become enlightened, and to seize opportunities to do that which defines us, our whole existence is elevated and our lives will be blessed with purpose, meaning, and happiness.

To create an insatiable appetite for learning is a key step toward the expansion of our minds. There is no better way to learn and expand our minds than the regular practiced habit of reading good literature. Getting into the hearts and thoughts of some of the world's great minds will assist each of us in our pursuits. Another powerful way to gain knowledge is through observation. As we watch, absorb, and apply information and skills, our minds will create new ways for us to achieve that which we seek. Writing is also a path toward exercising and expanding our minds, whether it is writing our thoughts in a diary or journal or using the written word in a professional capacity. The expansion of our minds empowers us with the opportunity to realize dreams and to transform a mundane life into a magnificent existence.

SPIRIT

Spirituality is a belief system that focuses on intangible elements that add meaning and vitality to our life experiences. It may be a belief in God, a dedicated prayer life, or communing with nature. In addition to believing in these intangible forces, personally experiencing these forces at work will add meaning to our lives. Spirituality is immensely personal. Each one of us personally chooses how we exemplify our spirituality. It may be outwardly obvious such as volunteering in our community or serving our church, or more internal such as searching for an inner sense of peace or developing our faith.

The concept of spirituality is not the intellectual property of any one religion or denomination. Our spirit, an inseparable third of the triad of body, mind, and spirit, belongs to each and every one of us. Pierre Teilhard de Chardin defined the importance of our spirituality by writing "We are not human beings having a spiritual experience. We are spiritual beings having a human experience." Developing our spirituality allows us to tap into the vast divine resource dwelling inside all of us and has the ability to release power and greatness beyond imagination. Becoming more spiritual allows us to eventually find that for which we are searching. As we begin to understand ourselves and our purposes, we will begin to walk the path toward purposeful happiness, and our flame will begin to burn bright for all to see. As our flame as well as the flames of others who are on the same path burn brightly as examples, our human consciousness is elevated to a more divine-like state.

The words spirit and inspire are derived from the same Latin root word, spirare, to breathe or blow. It is not a coincidence that when we are filled with spiritual energy, we are simultaneously filled with great inspiration.

So how do we become more spiritual? First, each individual must become aware of his or her spirituality and its intangible nature. Spirituality, like radio waves, is in the air and constantly surrounds us. They are both intangible; we cannot see, hear, or feel them. Unless we have a radio, a device that receives radio waves, the waves are useless.

Tapping into our vast incredible internal resources
with which we have been blessed
allows the expansion of spirituality.

The same goes for spirituality. We must develop the capacity to tune into the intangible—that is, things we cannot hold or see but need in order to live a life with purposeful happiness. Some of these intangibles are love, hope, and faith. One cannot hold or see these concepts, but we know when they are present because we can feel them and they make huge differences in our lives.

The second way to improve our spirituality is to experience the wonders of our Creator. Taking in the joyous wonder of a newborn baby, experiencing the vastness of a mountain range, staring up at billions of stars on a moonless night trying to comprehend the complexity of the universe, or enjoying the first tulips of spring as they arise from the cold earth bringing forth vibrant colors are all acts that will produce a spiritual experience if we have our spiritual radio tuned to the right frequency.

The third way to become more spiritual is to develop a daily routine through which we can each exercise our spirit. The routine is a personal and private matter for each of us to develop and to put into practice. Some common practices include prayer or meditation, reading of scripture or other reverent material, and other devotional efforts that invigorate the growth of intangibles such as love, hope, and faith.

The cosmic event would reach its pinnacle an hour before dawn. Isaac awoke early to gather his instruments so he could observe and record the glorious display. The coordinated dance between the heavenly bodies filled Isaac with a sense of awe. As he studied his observations and contemplated the movement of the celestial bodies, the sun began to rise over the tranquil countryside of Lincolnshire.

As Isaac sipped his tea and marveled at the splendor and magnificence of the sunrise, his mind wandered back to the amazing cosmic event that had unfolded just an hour earlier and he thought to himself, "What a wonderful day to be alive." The engagement in his worthy purpose of scientific discovery combined with his abundance of spiritual energy led Isaac to begin to comprehend complex, abstract concepts with ease. Enlightenment and understanding were flowing through Isaac when the ripe apple from a tree in his garden fell to the ground with the thud of discovery. The concept of gravity and its effects on the universe profoundly changed science and the world and produced purposeful happiness in the life of Sir Isaac Newton.

Combining spiritual awareness and energy with the pursuit of a passion will provide us with vision and insights and will create new possibilities. We may not discover a scientific breakthrough, but we will be heading toward purposeful happiness.

EIGHTH AXIOM OF HAPPINESS
THE TREE OF THREE... IN A NUTSHELL
To create happiness, care for your body, expand your mind, and become more spiritual.

NINTH
AXIOM OF HAPPINESS
Create a ripple
Give of yourself

———=•((◊))•=———

"There is a wonderful mythical law of nature
that the three things we crave most in life
—happiness, freedom, and peace of mind—
are always attained by giving them to someone else."
—Peyton Conway March—

The genuine giving of our time, energy, knowledge, and/or resources—without expectations—to others is the Ninth Axiom of Happiness. Generosity is rewarded in countless ways. We must each have faith that helping others is the right thing to do. Our giving without expectations will be rewarded in many and sometimes unexpected ways. It is written in 2 Corinthians 9:6–8, "⁶Remember this: Whoever sows sparingly will also reap sparingly, and whoever sows generously will also reap generously. ⁷Each man should give what he has decided in his heart to give, not reluctantly or under compulsion, for God loves a cheerful giver. ⁸And God is able to make all grace abound to you, so that in all things at all times, having all that you need, you will abound in every good work."

Help delivered is happiness received.

Care and concern for someone or something besides ourselves is a key element in producing happiness in our lives. The experience of happiness will come when we display selfless care and concern for our fellow human beings. Usually, we are more concerned about ourselves and are driven by our own personal motives and ambitions. The happiest people embrace the feelings, thoughts, and aspirations of others. "The most satisfying thing in life is to have been able to give a large part of ones' self to others" is how Pierre Teilhard de Chardin commented on this concept.

Becoming genuinely interested in the welfare of others is one of the crucial steps towards living with an abundance of happiness. Without sacrificing our own morals and core beliefs, it is important to be kind and tolerant of others, to be open to others' points of view and opinions, and to actively listen to their words and thoughts.

There is a way to begin giving that only requires a mental shift, a variation in our perspective. Although this shift will take time, energy, and awareness on our part, it will produce extremely positive results. If we can alter the way we listen and strive to listen to others with empathy, exciting changes will begin to appear to us and those around us. As we become adept at this valuable life skill, noticeable changes will begin to become apparent. Listening with empathy puts us in someone else's shoes; we begin to see the world as they do and to understand the way they feel. Empathic listening is listening without preparing to espouse our point of view, to tell what we think. It is listening with deep concentration and understanding to what the other person thinks. Listening with empathy can help each of us to forge a powerful connection with another person.

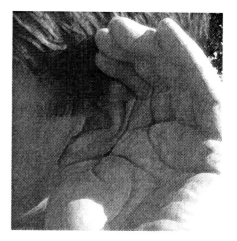

Hear words, absorb meaning.

Empathic listening, which is giving someone our complete undivided attention and becoming highly focused on a deep level of communication with another human spirit, will provide the one who is being heard with a great gift. This gift fulfills one of the greatest of human needs: the need to be appreciated, valued, and understood. Through the action of empathic listening, each of us will be led toward happiness. Sir John Templeton, best known for his philanthropy, has written "Happiness comes from spiritual wealth, not material wealth... Happiness comes from giving, not getting. If we try hard to bring happiness to others, we cannot stop it from coming to us also. To get joy, we must give it, and to keep joy, we must scatter it."

It is worthy to give gifts, especially if the action of giving is free of expectations of recompense or if, in giving, we are able to overcome selfishness. Giving of ourselves in order to help another and not because we expect something in return enhances our lives. Although we should not expect them, it is worthy to accept rewards or gifts gratefully when life presents them to us.

Giving is like throwing a stone into water. The ripples extend outward from the initial splash as does happiness from the original gift. The rippling effect from the act of giving will be noticed by others, which will result in additional stones of giving being thrown into the waters of life, thus creating even more ripples of happiness. These acts of giving and the resulting ripples of happiness can grow exponentially and eventually reach from shore to shore. Create a ripple: Give of yourself. Experience the happiness that results from the giving, and see the joy the giving brings to others.

Ripples

Throw a stone of giving
In the lake of living
See ripples grow
Ripples of happiness flow
As you give, the giving grows
The spirit of kindness goes and goes
The joy and happiness that you bring
In your life will also ring

August 8, 1991: It was a hot, humid Hoosier afternoon. Tom Weaver was in the gallery watching the PGA Championship at the Crooked Stick Golf Club in Carmel, Indiana. A severe thunderstorm blew in, and the warning signals blared urging all to seek shelter. Participants, officials, and fans headed for cover. Tom hustled back to the parking lot and the safety of his vehicle when, just a few feet away from it, he was struck in the chest by a bolt of lightning. In an instant, the 39-year-old husband and friend as well as father of 11-year-old Emily and 8-year-old Karen was gone.

John Daly was then a 25-year-old no-name in his first season on the PGA Tour. He was the ninth alternate with little hope of getting into the '91 PGA Championship field. Then, Nick Price withdrew because his wife went into labor, and three others ahead of Daly declined the last minute chance to play. Daly found himself in the field of the last major tournament of the season.

Daly's game of long, booming drives was well suited for Crooked Stick's long fairways. Daly soon became a fan favorite as he launched his massive drives, and he was within two shots of the lead after shooting a 69 the first day. Most rookies, as well as veterans, would have been elated to be within two shots of the lead in one of golf's major tournaments, but Daly's mood was somber due to the fact that a fan had been killed.

Daly continued playing well and finished with rounds of 67, 69, and 71 to win the tournament. For the win, he collected his first big paycheck of $230,000. After paying $175,000 on his house and $25,000 on his car, he had an idea for a special way to put to use the remaining money from his winnings.

A week after Tom's death, the family was notified that a trust had been established for the children's education. The trust was founded with $30,000, and the donor was John Daly. Even though Daly did not know the children's names, he wanted to help ease this tragic situation by providing assistance for their education.

The gift from Daly helped Emily to become a respiratory therapist, and Karen to graduate from Indiana University. Daly never followed up on his gift; he didn't want to bring up memories of that day when Emily and Karen's dad was killed. Fourteen years later, following Karen's graduation from college, the girls—now women—arranged to meet and personally thank Daly for his generosity and selfless gift. Daly's gift is an example of the ripple effect created by giving. His act created happiness for himself, even though personal happiness was not his motivation. Daly's gift also directly created happiness and opportunity for Tom Weaver's children. This single act of giving has and will continue to inspire countless other acts of kindness carried out by those whose lives' it has impacted as well as by those who have and will become aware of his example of generosity. He created a ripple.

John Daly's concern for others, exemplified in the funding the children's educational trust, is also a terrific example of the Fourth Axiom of Happiness—Do right, for it is right to do: Evaluate and understand motives. His thoughtful actions were selfless and were not undertaken in order to bring notoriety to himself. His quiet act of giving had a purity of cause. Norman MacEwan wrote these thoughts about giving and life: "Happiness is not so much in having as sharing. We make a living by what we get, but we make a life by what we give."

Create your own ripples. We can all make contributions that will help our fellow human beings, bring joy to ourselves, and help create a divine-like level of awareness. We all have the capacity and resources to give something back and to assist others.

True selfless giving is done without expectations. Others should be the focus of our giving, without thoughts of ourselves. John Daly did not expect something in return for funding the education for the children of the fan that died at the golf tournament. It was fourteen years after he created the ripple that his generosity was explicitly acknowledged by those directly impacted by his act of kindness. Daly was rewarded twice by his actions: first, by the contentment brought by doing the right thing and, second, by seeing and receiving the thanks of the two young women he helped with his gift.

Create a habit of giving. If each of us creates ripples of happiness with thoughtful acts, then we will have created an opportunity to experience purpose, meaning, and happiness in our lives.

THE PURSUIT: UP CLOSE AND PERSONAL

Dan, the unfulfilled designer/builder who uncovered his passion, had not been a habitual giver. He looked after himself and his family, but that was about the extent of his giving. Dan's metamorphosis from being unfulfilled to pursuing happiness included joining Habitat for Humanity and using his enormous talents in the building world to help create a home for a local family.

He also volunteered to teach a class about history and archaeology to interested senior citizens enrolled in the local continuing education program. His inner peace, contentment, and satisfaction also grew as he volunteered time and made regular donations at his church. Dan's motives were built on the necessary purity of cause, as he was doing these activities for the benefit of others. At the same time, a wonderful unexpected benefit was delivered to him as he became more fulfilled than at any time during his career as a designer/builder.

NINTH AXIOM OF HAPPINESS
CREATE A RIPPLE... IN A NUTSHELL

To create happiness, give to others without expectations and help others find happiness. Accept life's gifts graciously.

SYNOPSIS

We are creatures of habit. We gain comfort from the order of things. Our comfortable habits and patterns have taught us to receive an expected result if we produce a certain action. We get used to living in our comfortable patterns. However, if our usual routine is not fulfilling the gifts which are instilled within us, then we may be living a mundane existence. Because we are not living the life intended, our lives may feel empty as if something is missing. If we want to live a more fulfilling life—one with purpose, meaning, and happiness—then it is imperative that we change our current routine and begin to move toward that which defines us. When change is thrust upon us, we may feel a sense of fear or loss of control since our comfort zone has been disrupted. Transforming our dreams, goals, and desires into reality requires stepping out of our comfort zone, a move which may seem risky. However, the real risk is missing the opportunity to be or do that which defines us. We all are unique beings with talents, callings, and abilities waiting to be displayed. When we tap into our incredible internal reservoir of resources and begin to exercise our talents and to exhibit our gifts, we will find our lives moving from mundane to magnificent.

To transform our flickers to flames, to live with purpose, meaning, and happiness, we must believe we are in control of changing ourselves and our destinies. We have to have faith that we are capable of changing the way we think and act, and begin thinking and acting as if we are living our intended lives. However, there are a multitude of reasons why we don't embrace change and, as a result, miss the opportunity to exhibit our gifts: fear of failure, fear of success, lack of motivation, lack of commitment, lack of guidance, environment, and the list goes on and on. Everyone has obstacles to overcome to achieve goals, dreams, and callings, so we must minimize obstacles, embrace change, and achieve. Testing our mettle and pushing the limits of our potential should not be viewed as a fearful exercise, but rather as an experience that's fulfilling and exhilarating.

Life is constant change. Tomorrow we will be one day older than we are today, one day closer to the end of this existence. New relationships, experiences, and sensations emerge while the old ones creep away and eventually are forgotten. New souls are dawning while others are fading into the twilight of this life. The sun burns and is different today than it was yesterday, tectonic plates under the earth's mantle are constantly moving, mountains are eroding toward the oceans, and tomorrow the change of seasons is one day closer.

We are capable of fulfilling destiny and accomplishing dreams; if we can embrace change and break out of the ordinary, we will alter our lives forever. Beginning first with a devoted commitment to our goals and dreams, the development of the Nine Axioms of Happiness into a practiced way of life will lead us to the lives we have envisioned. The devoted commitment to achieving our goals or following our passions needs to be an unbreakable contract with ourselves, an ironclad Pact of Realization. Fulfillment of our goals and dreams will come true when we break out of our comfort zones, when we exchange our old, comfortable habits and patterns of just existing for the new, powerful, and effective Nine Axioms of Happiness. As we begin thinking with actions and acting with thoughts supplied by the Nine Axioms, the doors of possibility will be thrown open, and the metamorphosis from flicker to flame will have begun.

DIKEMBE MUTOMBO: A CASE IN POINT

Dikembe Mutombo had a humble beginning in the African country of Zaire, known now as the Democratic Republic of Congo. One of ten children, Dikembe was raised in poverty with his father earning only

$37 a month as a school master. His father was a strong role model and provided him with valuable life lessons like strength and perseverance.

Mutombo, with the aid of a scholarship, came to the United States to attend Georgetown University with plans to become a doctor and return home to help his fellow countrymen. During his second year at Georgetown, Mutombo, who was not hard to miss as he stands 7'2" tall, was recruited to play basketball by Coach John Thompson.

After a stellar basketball career at Georgetown and graduating with two bachelor degrees (one in Linguistics and one in Diplomacy), Mutombo, who also speaks seven languages, was selected as the fourth pick in the NBA draft. He has won numerous awards on the court in the NBA, including rookie of the year, all defensive team, defensive player of the year, and was named numerous times to the NBA all-star team.

Amazingly, his off the court accomplishments far outshine those on the court. Besides raising their own children, Mutombo and his wife Rose have adopted four nieces and nephews in an attempt to provide them with opportunities they would not otherwise have had. His actions have also extended outside the bounds of his own family. For example, he paid for the uniforms and expenses of the Zaire women's basketball team during the 1996 Olympics in Atlanta. In 1997, he created the Dikembe Mutombo Foundation to provide humanitarian assistance to his war-torn, poverty-stricken homeland. A few of the many awards he has received include USA Weekend Magazine's Most Caring Athlete Award, the Henry Iba Citizen Athlete Award, the President's Service Award, the Ernie Davis Humanitarian Award, and the J. Walter Kennedy Citizenship Award. In December 2001, ground was broken for a new hospital in Kinshasa, the capital of Congo. Mutombo has donated an astonishing $15 million dollars to this project in order to build the Biamba Marie Mutombo Hospital, named for his mother. Mutombo has said, "My father did so much for me that I want to have an impact on other people's lives." He has also said, "Maybe you can contribute to someone else's life, and they in turn can make a difference in so many others' lives.

We're here to help others help themselves." He obviously understands the concept of "create a ripple."

Let's examine how Dikembe Mutombo's thorough understanding of his gift and his passion, combined with his worthy purpose of generosity and wanting to help other people and the application of the concepts of the Nine Axioms of Happiness has and still is transforming his flicker to a flame that can be seen across continents.

FIRST AXIOM
Pack the wagon: Active actions
Mutombo has definitely packed the wagon. His actions speak loud and clear on both sides of the Atlantic Ocean. His active participation and generous actions in the arena of his passion are producing purposeful happiness in his life and in the lives of others. His actions are also creating a legacy that will continue to produce happiness for generations to come.

SECOND AXIOM
Believe it to be: Envision and prepare for the future
Mutombo's ambitious visions have been backed up with substantial efforts. Purposeful happiness is being realized, as his visions come to fruition with the efforts from today.

THIRD AXIOM
Make time to make it happen: Identify and limit distractions
Time is a precious commodity that distractions and obstacles try to steal from our worthy purpose. Imagine the discipline it would require to be the driving force behind building a hospital in Africa while living in the United States. Then add to that the rigorous demands of playing professional basketball in the NBA. Despite the demands of his professional career, Mutombo has found the concentration, focus, and time for his worthy purpose and is being rewarded with a life of purpose, meaning, and happiness.

FOURTH AXIOM
Do right, for it is right to do: Evaluate and understand motives

Mutombo's personification of the axiom "Do right, for it is right to do" is inspirational. His motives clearly contain the essential purity of cause. He is doing the right things for the right reasons by honoring his father and mother, generously helping and thinking of others, and moving away from selfishness and towards selflessness. The purposeful happiness being created is overwhelming.

FIFTH AXIOM
Receive inspiration, provide motivation:
Associate with fellow passion seekers

Mutombo was motivated by his father and mother who raised 10 children on $37 a month, provided their children an example of strength, and taught them valuable lessons. The inspiration Mutombo received from his parents is now being realized in the form of a new hospital. The family tie was the original association that provided inspiration and motivation. Mutombo learned well from his parents, and now he is the source of inspiration for others. For a project such as the Kinshasa hospital, a collection of inspired and motivated people had to be gathered. Purpose, meaning, and happiness are being realized not only by Mutombo but by all who are actively involved in making the dream come true.

SIXTH AXIOM
Pass it on: Teach others and express gratitude

The concept of "Pass it on" is wonderfully exhibited by Mutombo through the sharing of his resources. He is teaching the lessons of generosity and of helping others which will be heard for generations to come. Mutombo's actions are his way of thanking his parents and our Creator for the many blessings he has received; through these actions, he is leaving a tremendous legacy. Mutombo's reward of purposeful happiness is and will continue to be received.

SEVENTH AXIOM
Experience joy: Recognize and receive rewards

The Four Experiences of Profound Joy—epiphany, omni, golden moment, and reflection—are all capable of being received if there is an awareness of them. For Mutombo, an epiphany occurred when the idea for the hospital was born from the light possibility. Omni was present during the planning and building of the hospital: Everything seemed to be right, all the pieces of the puzzle seemed to miraculously come together, and the vision was beginning to be realized. The unexpected joyous events experienced during the passion quest are clearly golden moments. Finally, reflection will be experienced by Mutombo throughout his life, as he reminisces on his good deed and the difference he made to the people of his homeland.

EIGHTH AXIOM
The tree of three: Nurture body, mind, and spirit

Mutombo's care and concern for the triad of body, mind, and spirit has provided him with the energy necessary to compete in the world's highest level of professional basketball, with the knowledge and understanding to take advantage of the opportunities which have been presented to him, and with enlightenment produced by tapping into the vast, divine resource dwelling inside all of us.

NINTH AXIOM
Create a ripple: Give of yourself

Of all the Nine Axioms, "Create a ripple" is the one in which Mutombo's thoughts and actions shine brightest, providing all of us with an example of how giving of ourselves creates happiness. His flicker contains generosity and by maximizing that for which he was intended, he is living with purpose, meaning, and happiness. His generous actions, his flame which is visible across continents, has created ripples that will last for generations.

As you read and re-read this book, highlight the items that speak to you, the ones that you find important and meaningful and then re-read these sections. Consider *Flicker to Flame* a reference guide to a new, exciting way of life. Each time you re-read, you will reinforce what you have already learned, and perhaps discover a new idea or approach that you did not fully absorb previously. It takes time to integrate these concepts, these new ways of acting and thinking, into your life and to establish these new habits and patterns. Give yourself time as well as the proper foundation to build the magnificent life—which abounds with wonderful experiences—that you are intended to live.

Give several copies of this book to the people who are close to you, those who are in your sphere of influence: family, friends, acquaintances, or whoever needs assistance in their pursuit. You will be astonished at the life altering changes that will occur when you and those around you simultaneously put into practice the Nine Axioms.

One of the greatest gifts we can give someone is to teach them how to pursue happiness. This gift of love will allow them to create the life of their dreams, to fulfill their destiny, and to exhibit the greatness of their gifts.

Too many people live an ordinary existence and are unfulfilled. They never reach their potential and never unleash the beauty of their gifts. We all have the power within us to fulfill our dreams, to pursue happiness, to put our talents on display, and to be an example of what is possible. It requires work, energy, effort, and awareness of the Nine Axioms explored throughout this book to achieve a life packed full of purpose, meaning, and happiness. However, as Oliver Wendell Holmes wrote, "Many people die with their music still in them. Why is this so? Too often it is because they are always getting ready to live. Before they know it, time runs out." When we live life to the fullest extent by practicing the universal, natural laws of the Nine Axioms of Happiness, our music will be heard by the world.

I believe our Creator is the source of our conscience and of the universal principles and natural laws that govern our existence. As we each align our conscience with the universal principles and natural laws embodied in the Nine Axioms of Happiness, divinely inspired power and possibility will be released, allowing us to fulfill our destiny and exhibit to the world the gifts our Creator has provided.

To make the necessary, dramatic changes required to begin to follow our callings is the challenge before us. There is a way to get started living a life in which we will experience more purpose, meaning, and happiness: Read, understand, and do what is required for each of the following principles. Living life in accordance with the Nine Axioms of Happiness will create a personal road map for an outstanding life filled with contentment and enlightenment.

There is a prerequisite that is required prior to the implementations of the Nine Axioms. The first step, the genesis, is to have a clear vision of the goal or dream that is yearning for fulfillment.

GENESIS

Begin at the beginning: Evaluate and identify passions. Specifically write the definition of your vision. Don't just think about what it is you want to be or do. Don't keep it inside of you just as an idea. Clearly explain your vision in writing. If it is important enough to you, make it real by putting it down in writing.

Once the goal is etched into your being and the commitment is sealed with the Pact of Realization, it is time to begin putting into action the Nine Axioms described in the outline below.

NINE AXIOMS OF HAPPINESS

FIRST AXIOM
Pack the wagon: Active actions

List the activities and actions that are necessary and required to make your dream a reality. Begin to do what needs to be done.

SECOND AXIOM
Believe it to be: Envision and prepare for the future
Write a detailed description of the future. While visiting the future, describe what your life is like. What are you doing? What did you do to get there? Bring your vision of the future back to the present and start taking the necessary steps today to arrive at your perceived future.

THIRD AXIOM
Make time to make it happen: Identify and limit distractions
Create a list of the things holding you back from fulfilling your purpose. Prioritize the list of distractions or obstacles from the smallest (like convenient excuses) to what you perceive to be the largest. Start eliminating or minimizing the distractions starting with the largest ones and allocate more time to your passion.

FOURTH AXIOM
Do right, for it is right to do: Evaluate and understand motives
Create a list of why you are going to pursue this passion from the most to least important. Share your thoughts with your confidant, the person closest to you. Attempt to grow and move from selfish to selfless.

FIFTH AXIOM
Receive inspiration, provide motivation:
Associate with fellow passion seekers
Create a list of people who you believe are following their dreams, who are living life on their terms both in and out of your area of pursuit. Make a concentrated effort to meet and become friends, associates, or protégés of these people. Study and learn from them. Apply the appropriate lessons to your life.

SIXTH AXIOM
Pass it on: Teach and express gratitude
As you become actively involved in fulfilling your destiny, assist others in the quest of their dreams. Communicate with mentors, the people who have assisted in your pursuit. Express gratitude and keep them informed of your progress.

SEVENTH AXIOM
Experience joy: Recognize and receive rewards
Be prepared to recognize, accept, and enjoy the rewards of following your dreams.

EIGHTH AXIOM
The tree of three: Nurture body, mind and spirit
Make three lists—one for the body, the mind, and the spirit—of specific activities that you will engage in to nourish these three important aspects of you. Be active in improving all three areas.

NINTH AXIOM
Create a ripple: Give of yourself
Specifically list activities and organizations in which you will be involved in giving something back. Change your attitude and behavior and become more giving.

If the necessary time and effort is taken to read, understand, and prepare the outline described above, a personal road map to a happy, fulfilled, and content life will have been created. The game plan for a successful life will need to be adjusted, updated, and improved as situations change and more understanding and enlightenment is gained.

The above suggestion for creating an outline will work for some. However, as mentioned numerous times in this book, we are all unique beings with different skills and talents, and how we learn and apply information will vary greatly. How you create your game plan is really up to you. It is not how you implement the Nine Axioms of Happiness—whether you create an outline or begin implementing the axioms as opportunities arise, since ultimately it is a personal choice—but *if* you implement the axioms and turn them into a way of life. We all possess the capabilities to live a joyful life filled with happiness. I hope that *Flicker to Flame* will be able to serve as a reference guide for the voyage.

To fulfill purpose and answer a calling, courage to become proficient in practicing the Nine Axioms of Happiness is required. Significant, life-altering changes will result as the axioms become practiced habits. If the people that surround us—family, friends, employees, co-workers, or fellow members of organizations—learn and begin practicing the Nine Axioms of Happiness, it will create a culture of limitless possibilities.

Just imagine if everyone around us was engaged in actively pursuing their passion. If this vision of supportive people who help others fulfill their dreams while thanking those who assisted them, who give back and contribute to the greater good of society, who visualize joy, who are void of distractions, who continually refresh and expand their bodies, minds, and spirits, who let their conscience be their guide, and who experience happiness, came to fruition, the world would abound in peace and prosperity. The world would be a much different place than it is today, and our human existence would be greatly altered from what it is now. I believe the inspiration for this book was given to me to help create such a world by helping individuals create the life of their dreams, pursue their purpose, and become an outward example of their inner greatness. I hope the message contained in *Flicker to Flame* is received, that it will help each of us exhibit what great gifts we all have been given, and that we ultimately give credit to our Creator for such wonderful gifts.

INDEX OF QUOTES

Inspiration and motivation are delivered and received in many varied forms. When recorded in the written form, important, thought-provoking ideas are capable of becoming memorable quotes. I have compiled the quotes used in the book—some famous, some not so famous—that particularly helped me express or reiterate an idea or concept. The quotes are listed alphabetically by author. The compilation of quotes serves as an extension of the book and has the same purpose: to provide a sense of direction toward the understanding that we possess the power to live the magnificent life intended, to help dreams become reality, and to remember to give thanks to our Creator for our blessings.

QUOTES

"Happiness is the meaning and purpose of life, the whole aim and the end of human existence"
—Aristotle, ancient Greek philosopher, scientist, and physician, 384–322 BC

"Gratitude unlocks the fullness of life. It turns what we have into enough, and more. It turns denial into acceptance, chaos to order, confusion to clarity. It can turn a meal into a feast, a house into a home, a stranger into a friend. Gratitude makes sense of our past, brings peace for today, and creates a vision for tomorrow."
—Melody Beattie, American author

"⁶We have different gifts, according to the grace given us. If a man's gift is prophesying, let him use it in proportion to his faith. ⁷If it is serving, let him serve; if it is teaching, let him teach; ⁸If it is encouraging, let him encourage; if it is contributing to the needs of others, let him give generously; if it is leadership, let him govern diligently; if it is showing mercy, let him do it cheerfully."
—The Bible, Romans 12:6–8

"Let your light shine before men that they may see your good works and give glory to your father who is in heaven."
—The Bible, Matthew 5:16

"I know that there is nothing better for men than to be happy and do good while they live."
—The Bible, Ecclesiastes 3:12

"³Trust in the Lord and do good; dwell in the land and enjoy safe pasture. ⁴Delight yourself in the Lord and he will give you the desires of your heart."
—The Bible, Psalm 37:3–4

"⁶Remember this: Whoever sows sparingly will also reap sparingly, and whoever sows generously will also reap generously. ⁷Each man should give what he has decided in his heart to give, not reluctantly or under compulsion, for God loves a cheerful giver. ⁸And God is able to make all grace abound to you, so that in all things at all times, having all that you need, you will abound in every good work."
—The Bible, 2 Corinthians 9:6–8

"It's the constant and determined effort that breaks down resistance, sweeps away all obstacles."
—Claude M. Bristol, American author and speaker, 1891–1951

"All that we are is the result of what we have thought. If a man speaks or acts with an evil thought, pain follows him. If a man

speaks or acts with a pure thought, happiness follows him, like a shadow that never leaves him."
—Buddha, Hindu Prince Gautama Siddharta, founder of Buddhism, 563–483 BC

"To keep the body in good health is a duty, otherwise we shall not be able to keep our mind strong and clear."
—Buddha

"There is work that is work, and there is play that is play; there is play that is work, and work that is play. And in only one of these lies happiness."
—Gelett Burgess, American artist, art critic, poet, author, and humorist, 1866–1951

"We are not human beings having a spiritual experience. We are spiritual beings having a human experience."
—Pierre Teilhard de Chardin, French geologist, priest, and philosopher, 1881–1955

"The most satisfying thing in life is to have been able to give a large part of ones' self to others."
—Pierre Teilhard de Chardin

"I believe that the very purpose of our life is to seek happiness. That is clear. Whether one believes in religion or not, whether one believes in this religion or that religion, we all are seeking something better in life. So, I think, the very motion of our life is towards happiness... "
—Dalai Lama, the head of the Dge-lugs-pa order of Tibetan Buddhists, winner 1989 Nobel Peace Prize

"Only passions, great passions can elevate the soul to great things."
—Denis Diderot, French man of letters and philosopher, 1713–1784

"Action may not always bring happiness, but there is no happiness without action."
—Benjamin Disraeli, British prime minister and novelist, 1804–1881

"Imagination is your preview of life's coming attractions."
—Albert Einstein, German-born American physicist who developed the special and general theories of relativity and received the Nobel Prize for Physics 1921, 1879–1955

"It is never too late to be what you might have been."
—George Eliot, English Victorian novelist, pseudonym of Mary Ann Evans, 1819–1880

"We must not cease from exploration. And the end of all our exploring will be to arrive where we began and to know the place for the first time."
—T.S. Eliot, American born English editor, playwright, poet, and critic, 1888–1965

"It is one of the most beautiful compensations of this life that no man can sincerely try to help another without helping himself."
—Ralph Waldo Emerson, American poet, lecturer, and essayist, 1803–1882

"If you wish to live a life free from sorrow, think of what is going to happen as if it had already happened."
—Epictetus, Greek philosopher associated with the Stoics, AD 55–c.135

"Work is love made visible. And if you cannot work with love but only with distaste, it is better that you should leave your work and sit at the gate of the temple and take alms of those who work with joy."
—Kahil Gibran, Lebanese born American philosophical essayist, novelist, and poet, 1883–1931

"Whatever you can do or dream you can, begin it. Boldness has genius, power, and magic in it."
—Johann Wolfgang von Goethe, German playwright, poet, novelist, and dramatist, 1749–1832

"Treat people as if they were what they ought to be, and you help them to become what they are capable of being."
—Johann Wolfgang von Goethe

"Many people die with their music still in them. Why is this so? Too often it is because they are always getting ready to live. Before they know it, time runs out."
—Oliver Wendell Holmes, American physician, poet, writer, humorist, and professor at Harvard, 1809–1894

"Carpe diem, quam minimum credula postero." Latin for, "Seize the day, put no trust in tomorrow."
—Horace, ancient Roman poet, 65–8 BC

"Happiness, though an indefinite concept, is the goal of all rational beings."
—Immanuel Kant, German philosopher, considered the last major philosopher from the Age of Enlightenment, 1724–1804

"Joy is the holy fire that keeps our purpose warm and our intelligence aglow."
—Helen Keller, American author and educator who was blind and deaf, 1880–1968

"When one door of happiness closes, another opens; but often we look so long at the closed door that we do not see the one which has been opened for us."
—Helen Keller

"Let no feeling of discouragement prey upon you, and in the end you are sure to succeed."
—Abraham Lincoln, 16th President of the United States of America, 1809–1865

"Confidence is contagious. So is lack of confidence."
—Vince Lombardi, American football coach, 1913–1970

"Happiness is not so much in having as sharing. We make a living by what we get, but we make a life by what we give."
—Norman MacEwan, Canadian prime minister, 1891–1951

"There is a wonderful mythical law of nature that the three things we crave most in life—happiness, freedom, and peace of mind— are always attained by giving them to someone else."
—Peyton Conway March, American general and Army Chief of Staff, 1864–1955

"If people knew how hard I worked to get my mastery, it wouldn't seem so wonderful after all."
—Michelangelo, Italian sculptor, painter, architect, and poet, considered the creator of the Renaissance, 1475–1564

"Pay any price to stay in the presence of extraordinary people."
—Mike Murdock, American minister, author, songwriter, poet, and philosopher

"What you leave behind is not what is engraved in stone monuments, but what is woven into the lives of others."
—Pericles, ancient Greek politician and general, 495–429 BC

"Not everyone aspires to be a bank president or a nuclear scientist, but everybody wants to do something with one's life that will give him pride and a sense of accomplishment."
—Ronald Reagan, 40th President of the United States of America, 1911–2004

"I invent nothing; I rediscover."
—Auguste Rodin, French sculptor, 1840–1917

"You are the average of the five people you spend the most time with."
—Jim Rohn, American speaker and author

"We cannot hold a torch to light another's path without brightening our own.
—Ben Sweetland, American author

"Happiness comes from spiritual wealth, not material wealth... Happiness comes from giving, not getting. If we try hard to bring happiness to others, we cannot stop it from coming to us also. To get joy, we must give it, and to keep joy, we must scatter it."
—Sir John Templeton, American born British philanthropist

"Go confidently in the directions of your dreams. Live the life you have imagined."
—Henry David Thoreau, American essayist, poet, and philosopher, 1817–1862

"The secret of happiness is freedom. The secret of freedom is courage."
—Thucydides, an ancient Greek historian and author, 460–404 BC

"Body and mind, and spirit, all combine to make the Creature, human and divine."
—Ella Wheeler Wilcox, American poet and writer, 1850–1919

"Laugh, and the world laughs with you. Weep and you weep alone..."
—Ella Wheeler Wilcox

"If you observe a really happy man you will find him building a boat, writing a symphony, educating his son, growing double dahlias in his garden, or looking for dinosaur eggs in the Gobi desert. He will not be searching for happiness as if it were a collar button that has rolled under the radiator. He will not be striving for it as a goal in itself. He will have become aware that he is happy in the course of living life twenty-four crowded hours of the day."
—W. Beran Wolfe, Australian psychiatrist and author, 1900–1935

THE NINE AXIOMS OF HAPPINESS
IN ACTION

—————⟨●⟩—————

To live with purpose, meaning, and happiness the Nine Axioms of Happiness need to move beyond theory and be put into practice. In my implementation of the Nine Axioms, I met a dedicated passion seeker, Dr. Chuck Dietzen, founder and president of the Timmy Foundation. Dr. Chuck and I share a vision of making a difference in the world one person at a time. My association with the Timmy Foundation is a practical application of the Nine Axioms of Happiness which allows my actions to speak as loudly as my words.

I am donating a portion of the proceeds from the sale of this book to the foundation. If you would like to get involved with a wonderful, caring organization dedicated to improving the medical and educational opportunities of children around the world, contact the Timmy Foundation. Thank you for your support.

TIMMY FOUNDATION

Our Vision is a world in which basic healthcare and education are available to all children.

Our Mission is to build healthy futures worldwide, one child at a time. We accomplish this by strengthening community-based health and education initiatives and empowering young people to share their energy and compassion. To carry out our mission, we organize international service trips, for which we collect and distribute appropriate medicines, medical equipment and supplies, and funding and educational materials to projects in Ecuador, Haiti, Colombia, Nigeria, South Africa, Jamaica, Dominican Republic, Honduras, and the U.S.A.

Visit our website for more information: www.timmyfoundation.org

"We were not all born to be doctors and nurses, but we were all born to be healers."
—Dr. Chuck Dietzen

"It is not my job to be successful. It is my job to be faithful."
—Mother Teresa

SPECIAL OPPORTUNITY
The simultaneous reading of *Flicker to Flame* and the implementation of the Nine Axioms of Happiness by a group such as a company, school, organization, team, or church can produce amazing positive results by creating a culture of happiness and joy. I, and the publisher Morgan James Publishing, strongly believe in this culture of happiness and joy and the uplifting effect it has on the individual as well as the group involved. We, author and publisher, have set up special group discounts for the purchase of *Flicker to Flame* to facilitate the culture of happiness and joy in groups that wish to participate. To get more information or to make a discounted group purchase go to www.jeffrey-t-parker.com/groupdiscounts.html

CONTACT INFORMATION
Jeff and his wife Laura, to whom he has been happily married for twenty years, have three children, Rachel, Jessica, and Ryan, and live in Bloomington, Indiana. Jeff may be reached at:

P.O. Box 313, Clear Creek, IN 47426

Phone: 812.824.5676

E-mail: jparker44@hotmail.com

Web site: jeffrey-t-parker.com

Printed in the United States
68851LVS00004BA/17

9 781600 371073